Routledge Revivals

Japanese Traditions of Christianity

Japanese Traditions of Christianity

M. Paske-Smith

Routledge
Taylor & Francis Group

First published by Kegan Paul, Trench, Trübner & Co., Ltd.

This edition first published in 2018 by Routledge
2 Park Square, Milton Park, Abingdon, Oxon, OX14 4RN
and by Routledge
711 Third Avenue, New York, NY 10017

Routledge is an imprint of the Taylor & Francis Group, an informa business

Publisher's Note
The publisher has gone to great lengths to ensure the quality of this reprint but points out that some imperfections in the original copies may be apparent.

Disclaimer
The publisher has made every effort to trace copyright holders and welcomes correspondence from those they have been unable to contact.

A Library of Congress record exists under ISBN: 31010789

ISBN 13: 978-1-138-60443-8 (hbk)

ISBN 13: 978-1-138-60493-3 (pbk)

ISBN 13: 978-0-429-46233-7 (ebk)

The ordinary edition of this book comprised one thousand copies, of which this is one.

There was also an edition of twenty-five numbered copies printed on hand-made paper.

Picture of the Fighting at Shimabara, reproduced from the *Shimabara Kassen-ki*

JAPANESE

TRADITIONS OF CHRISTIANITY

BEING SOME OLD TRANSLATIONS FROM THE JAPANESE, WITH BRITISH CONSULAR REPORTS OF THE PERSECUTIONS OF 1868-1872

EDITED BY

M. PASKE-SMITH C.B.E., H.B.M. CONSUL, OSAKA.

WITH JAPANESE NOTES
BY
SHUTEN INOUYE

J. L. THOMPSON & CO. (RETAIL) LTD.,
KOBE, JAPAN.

KEGAN PAUL, TRENCH, TRUBNER, & CO. LTD.,
LONDON.

List of Contents

CONTENTS—*(Continued)*

CONTENTS—*(Continued)*

LIST OF ILLUSTRATIONS

Japanese Traditions of Christianity.

THE story of the introduction of Christianity into Japan in the sixteenth century is a fascinating study. From 1549, when St. Francis Xavier, named the Apostle of the East, landed at Kagoshima in Satsuma, until 1640 Roman Catholic missionaries made ceaseless and heroic efforts to convert the Japanese nation. The ruling classes were at first inclined to tolerate, if not welcome, the new religion. In 1552 Otomo Hachiro (大友八郎), later known as Ouchi Yoshinaga (大內義長) Lord of Yamaguchi, presented the missionaries with a Temple and lands. A facsimile of this grant was found by the late Sir Ernest Satow in a book published at Cologne in 1574 and was translated by him as follows :—

> "With respect to Daidoji (*i.e.* monastery of the great way) in Yamaguchi, Province of Suwo. This deed witnesses that I have given permission to the priests who have come to this country from western regions, in accordance with their request and desire that they may found and erect a monastery and house in order to develop the law of Buddha.
>
> "28th day of the 8th month of 21st year Tenbun Era (September 16th 1552).[1] "

---

1 See Transactions Asiatic Soc. Japan Vol. VII.

At first, therefore, Christianity was taken to be nothing more than a superior form of Buddhism but as its power increased the rulers of Japan grew afraid that its aims were other than spiritual, and its teachings came to be banned. The first to issue a national edict of banishment against the Catholic priests was Toyotomi Hideyoshi in 1587 ; ten years later he repeated the edict more rigorously and, no doubt, had he not died in 1598 he would have taken steps to see that the priests actually did leave the land. But his death gave a respite and it was not until 1614 that his successor, Tokugawa Iyeyasu, was moved to order the deportation of all missionaries. In that year the last Christian Religious Procession* for over 250 years took place in Nagasaki. Between 1614 and 1640 the persecution became every year more severe until finally the country was closed to all foreigners except the Chinese and the Dutch.

Owing to the rigour with which all native documents, pictures and letters were systematically destroyed at the time of the persecutions, there are hardly any contemporary records of Christianity from the Japanese side. Historians have had to depend largely on the annual letters and reports which it was customary for the Jesuits and other missionaries to send home to their principals in Europe and India. Consequently such Japanese accounts as do exist are traditional rather than historical, being nearly all written at least one hundred years after the events recorded. The best known are the Real Record of the Arrival of Christianity in Japan (Kirisutan Shumon Raicho Jikki 切支丹宗門來朝實記), the Record of the Rise and Fall of the Temple of the Southern Barbarians (Nambanji Kohai Ki 南蠻寺興廢記) and the Record of the Origin of Christianity (Kirisutan Kongen Ki 切支丹根元記).

The Real Record of the Arrival of Christianity in Japan was written by an anonymous author in the 5th year of the Horeki (寶暦) era or A.D. 1755, that is over a century after the final expulsion of the foreign Roman Catholic Priests. The translation which forms Part I of this book corresponds for

* For route of this procession see map at end of the book.

the most part with the text of the Record; it appeared in the *Japan Herald* of 1864 but the name of the translator is unknown.

At first sight this and other traditional Japanese tales of Christianity appear to be wildly inaccurate but closer examination shows them to contain, tinged with tradition, some well established facts. Chief of these seems to be that Christianity was exterminated not so much on religious as on political grounds. As already mentioned, the first ruler of Japan to initiate the persecution was Toyotomi Hideyoshi, the Regent of Japan from 1583 to 1598. Until 1587 missionary accounts report the receipt of innumerable favours from Hideyoshi but in that year his attitude changed completely. The classic reason always given by historians for his fury against the Christian religion and his martyrdom of the Twenty-six Saints at Nagasaki on the 5th February 1597 is the statement made by the pilot of a Spanish galleon, the "San Felipe," which, after taking refuge in a Japanese port, had been seized by the orders of the Regent who, it is said, coveted her rich cargo. The pilot desirous to save his ship and cargo, attempted to overawe the Japanese authorities by describing the might of Spain and, in reply to a question as to how his king came to possess so many lands, said that the method adopted was to begin by sending into the countries he wanted to conquer priests, who induced the people to embrace the Catholic religion and, when they had made considerable progress, to send troops who, combined with the new Christians, had little trouble in accomplishing the rest.

This statement of the Pilot of the "San Felipe" had, as we know, a certain element of truth in it. But judging from old Spanish manuscripts lately made available (see Catalogue of Maggs Bros. Bibliotheca Asiatica, Part III.), the Japanese had, besides this verbal information, an example of Spain's predatory religious methods at their doors. This was the Spanish expedition sent from Manila in 1596 to assist the King of

Cambodia against the King of Champan or Champa (占 波) (Annam). In the body of the Record references are made to the success attending mission work in " China " which terminated in the conquest of the land. As this is contrary to history an examination was made of the original Japanese text from which it became clear that the translator mistook the characters " 占 國 " to mean " China " whereas these characters in olden times were used by the Japanese to denote the Kingdom of Champan or Champa which included roughly the valley of the River Mekong. According to an old manuscript the King of Cambodia sent to Manila a Spaniard, Don Diego de Veloso, asking Spanish assistance against the King of Champa. At a conference between the Ambassadors of the King and the Governor-General, the Archbishop and other Royal Spanish Officials it was decided that the aid asked should be given provided that the King embraced the Catholic Faith and permitted Catholic priests to enter his Kingdom freely ; that the Spaniards were given a port and suitable land for colonisation ; that the King paid all the expenses of the expedition and took an oath to be faithful to the King of Spain ; that in the event of success against Champa that country was to be divided between Spain and Cambodia ; that pagan worship was forbidden ; and finally that the King consulted the Spaniards as to his successor. In other words the country was to be practically ceded to Spain. Another writer in Manila at the same period, summing up a description of Champa, considered it to be one of the most important strategical positions in the East and declared it could be conquered and maintained by one hundred and fifty Spaniards with five hundred local troops. In the sixteenth century Japanese junks used to trade regularly to the Philippines, Siam, Cambodia, Champan and Cochin China, so that news of these preparations must certainly have been carried back to Japan and, although the Spanish expedition which left Manila in 1596 did not meet with complete success, its operations in Champa and Cambodia were no doubt fully reported. It is easy therefore to understand how ready credence was given to the words of the pilot of the " San Felipe " and how the story of the successful use of religious penetration into Champa became current in Japan.

But besides the above incidents the Japanese authorities had had other disquietening reports on the political possiblities of Christianity from Japanese, who accompanied Catholic Priests to Europe and Mexico. There was the Embassy to the Pope from the Princes of Kyushu whose members returned in 1591. In 1614 the Daimyo of Sendai, Date Masamune, also sent an Envoy to His Holiness through Mexico and Spain. In 1622 Ibi Masayoshi, a Tokugawa official, who had been sent abroad by Iyeyasu Tokugawa in 1615, returned and his report could have been anything but reassuring. The Dutch and English merchants who reached Japan in 1609 and 1613 respectively also lost no opportunity of impressing on Japanese officialdom the dangers to be apprehended from Roman Catholicism. Is it then a matter for wonder that the Japanese linked Christianity with aggression and that its followers came to be regarded as political rebels !

Corollary to this dread of conquest are the warnings given in the " Record " against the insiduous methods said to have been adopted by the missionaries to gain the converts, who were subsequently to assist in the overthrow of their own land. By assisting the needy, comforting the poor, healing the sick—all Christian traits—but, as we shall see, suspect in the eyes of Japanese officials in ancient times. From the missionaries themselves we learn how at first they attempted to convert by humility and works of charity but were compelled, for want of success, to clothe themselves in fine raiment and seek out the rich nobles, for, with their conversion, that of their followers was easy. Hence the " Record " tells how Christianity began to dazzle the nobility until it endangered the realm. As the man who exposed his country to these dangers, Oda Nobunaga, the predecessor of Hideyoshi, is held up in the " Record " as the villain while Hideyoshi is shown as the national hero who saw through the cunning wiles of the missionaries to dominate the land preparatory to the introduction of a foreign army of conquest.

PART I.

A History of the Introduction of Christianity into Japan.

(TRANSLATED FROM THE JAPANESE).

We find, on examining the history of Christianity, that it was first brought to Japan in the 11th year of the reign of Ogimachi, the 107th Emperor, and in the time of Nobunaga.[1]

This Nobunaga being an unprincipled and perverse man, tore down the Shinto and Buddhist temples and seized their possessions. His obstinate and unrestrained conduct were so great, the good protecting gods, we may suppose, turned away their eyes. The devil, taking advantage of this opportunity to introduce false doctrines and wicked rites, brought over this religion, whereby an unknown multitude of people were destroyed.

This Christianity is a wicked religion that came from the country of Namban.

---

1 The 11th year of the reign of Ogimachi, that is the 11th year of the Eiroku era (1558-1570) or A.D. 1568. At the time the Ashikaga Family was in power in Japan, the name of the ruling Shogun being Yoshihide (義榮) who was succeeded in the same year by Yoshiaki (義昭).

Christianity was first introduced into Japan by St. Francis Xavier, the Apostle of the East, who landed at Kagoshima in Southern Japan in 1549, but the date 1568 corresponds with the time that it began to become popular in Kyoto, the Capital, under the protection of Oda Nobunaga, who ruled in Japan from 1565 to 1582 at first in the name of Ashikaga Yoshiaki (足利義昭) but later in his own. It is said that he allowed the introduction of Christianity under the impression that it was only another sect or form of Buddhism, which had also come over from India, the country from which St. Francis first came to Japan; but it is far more probable that he saw in Christianity a weapon to aid him in overcoming the overpowering influence which the Buddhist priesthood was obtaining in Japanese politics. By giving his support to this new cult he hoped to draw from Buddhism, as he did, many of the influential supporters of his enemies among the Buddhist priests.

This Namban[2] is bounded on the West by India, on the South by the country of Ume,[3] on the North by Shoku,[4] and on the East by the Ocean. It is 33,000 miles square and has 42 provinces. It is in a S.W. direction from Japan, and distant by sea more than 12,000 miles. The name of the King was Gojimbi.[5]

On a certain time the King assembled all his lords, and said: "On the N.E. of this country there is a small country called Japan; all kinds of merchandize are shipped to it from India and Holland. It appears to be a country abounding in gold and silver. If we could only seize, and get possession of it, it would promote the prosperity of our own country and enrich the people; how do you think this can be accomplished?"

Then Tenriki,[6] the General of the right, whose height was nine feet, his colour black, hair red, and voice like the sound of a large bell, advancing, said: "I understand your Majesty's intention; nothing could be easier, (*lit.* it is in the

---

2 In ancient times China considered all culture and civilisation to be centred in herself; all others were barbarians, divided into Eastern Barbarians (Toi, 東夷) which included even the Japanese, Western Barbarians (Seiju, (西戎), Northern Barbarians (Hokuteki, 北狄), and Southern Barbarians (Namban, 南蠻). In the last were included the Portuguese and Spaniards who arrived in Japan from the South. This term Namban covered roughly those countries which nowadays are known to the Japanese as Nanyo, that is Siam, Malaya, Philippines, Dutch East Indies and Cochin China.

3 Ume. In the "Real Record" the Japanese characters (烏馬) are used for this country but in the frequent copying of the manuscript the first character (烏) may possibly have been miswritten for (鳥), cho, which, with the second character pronounced "ba", as is permissible, would give "Choba", indicating Java.

4 Shoku (蜀). This is a geographical term given formerly to Szechuan Province and included also perhaps Yunnan.

5 Gojimbi (合志尾). In another Japanese manuscript Kai-shu-pi is given and refers no doubt to King Philip of Spain.

6 **Tenriki (天力).** In the "Real Record" the characters (呑力) Donriki **appear but may be a transliteration for Tenriki (天力) meaning "Heavenly Power".**

palm of my hand) than to collect a large army in a few days, cross over and conquer Japan, and thus accomplish your Majesty's desire of making it a dependency of Namban."

The Emperor was greatly rejoiced and said: "Go, then, take a large army, cross over to that country, and carry out my wishes." But Goki,[7] the General of the left, contracting his eyebrows, said: "What General Tenriki has advised is not good, because Japan has frequently, before this, been attacked by some of the 42 provinces of Namban; but, in not a single instance have they gained a victory. Senkotei[8] also, the General of Hokuteki, (*lit.* Northern barbarians), made war upon Japan, but being the country of the Gods, and under their powerful protection, he also, as well as Namban, though they have invaded Japan seven times, has always been defeated. Now it is my opinion that we should do, as we did in the case of China,[9] send thither

---

7 Goki (吳輝) or Koki (巨喜) in another manuscript.

8 Senkotei (泉向帝) and Hokuteki (北狄). This must refer to the attempt of Kublai Khan and the Mongols to invade Japan in 1274 and 1281, which was defeated owing to the energy of Hojo Tokumine, the de facto ruler of Japan at the time.

9 China. In the Japanese original the characters are (占國) Senkoku, which was the name given by the Japanese to the Kingdom of Champa or Tshiampa and sometimes Champan. The translator of the pamphlet has obviously mistranslated these characters as "China". The Jesuits did not enter China until after their expulsion from Japan but they are known to have been at work in Champa previous to 1600. In 1596 the Spaniards sent a military expedition to Champa from Manila to aid the King of Cambodia in its conquest in which they were to share the spoils. The departure of this expedition and its arrival in Annam must certainly have become known to the Japanese by means of their trading junks, which used to trade regularly to Champa (Annam) and Cambodia. In later years Richard Cocks, who directed English trade in Japan from 1613 to 1623 often mentions the arrival of Japanese junks from Champa. As mentioned in the introduction it is more than probable that the news of Spain's attempted mastery of Champa was one of the contributory causes for Hideyoshi's (Ruler of Japan 1583-1598) sudden persecution of Christianity in 1597 after he had tacitly allowed his previous edict of 1887 to lapse.

persons proficient in religious discipline, who shall bring them into subjection by means of religious rites, and give money to those who are poor and afflicted. After we have, in this way, gained over one-third of the people, then sending an army of a few thousand men, with the assistance of those who are obedient to us, there is no doubt but that we should obtain the victory over them. We should not enter upon it with too much haste; let us reflect well upon it."

The Emperor, nodding, said: "What General Tenriki said was certainly reasonable, but what the General of the left has just said, is exceedingly judicious. Let the great lords of the left and right mature a good plan."

When the inquiry was made as to what kind of a proficient in religion it should be that should be sent to Japan, the General of the left said:

"About one thousand miles to the west of this, is what are called the Tenrin mountains.[10] In these mountains is a place called Christian. (*Jap.* ke-restan). Here are two religious devotees excelling in doctrine and miraculous power. One of them is called Padre Urugan,[11] the other Padre Furaten. They are both priests, who having practiced holy contemplation, can at pleasure, ascend into the air, without approaching the sky, or touching the earth. They can make it rain, and cause the wind to blow. From the possession of this miraculous power, their name of padre (*Jap.* Ba-te-ren) is derived, Ba meaning to rend; Te, contraction of Ten the heavens, and Ren, to pass

10 Tenrin mountains. For this word in the Japanese text is Tenringan (天輪岸) or Heaven-wheel-rocks. In another manuscript of the Nambanji Kohai Ki (南蠻寺興廢記) it is Tenrinho (天林峯) or Heaven Forest Peak.

11 Urugan (宇留岸) and Furuten (富羅天). It is probable that these two names are meant for Fathers Organtino Gnecchi and Luis Froez who were the best known priests at Kyoto in the days of Nobunaga; Froez was there from 1568 and Organtino from 1872. It is, of course, possible that the reference may be to Velignani, the Jesuit Visitor-General, who was also a frequent visitor to Kyoto where he always excited much interest on account of his height; in fact, from his "inches" arose no doubt the tradition of the tallness of the Fathers mentioned in the Record.

through the clouds. On this account they are called Bateren; this is the origin of the sect of the Bateren.[12] Besides these there is a person called Raman (*Jap.* Iruman).[13] He is a disciple of the others. If by means of foreign religion and miraculous powers the people of Japan are brought into submission, your Majesty's desire will of course be attained."

The Emperor was greatly rejoiced, and said: "Who shall we send to the Tenriki mountains?" Goki replied, "My son Goga[14] may be sent." So Goga went to the country of Christian in the Tenriki mountains. After enquiring here and there, he at last found Urugan. Goga, addressing him in the most respectful language, said: "Reverend Sir, I have come to you on a message from the Kindgom of Namban. The great King of that country requests your assistance; I pray you therefore to come without delay to his capital. "Urugan, hearing, said: "What can His Majesty want with such an one as me, a hermit of the mountains?" Goga replied: "Reverend Sir, your eminent virtues cannot be hid. His Majesty wishes to send you to Japan, for the purpose of gaining the hearts of the people, and spreading abroad your religious arts." Urugan, hearing, said: "I am a person of no talents, and am not able to go to Japan to spread abroad my arts; return and tell this to the great King." So saying he vanished. Goga was greatly surprised, and not wishing to return in this way, he searched about; but on every side a cloud covered him, so that he could not see where he was going. Having therefore nothing left for him to do, he returned to the capital of Namban, and reported the matter.

Goki said: "I think it has turned out thus, because we have been sparing of our presents to the Padre; if we once

---

12 Bateren is more likely to be a Japanese corruption of the Spanish word "Padre"; in fact this is its generally accepted derivation.

13 Roman or Iruman (伊留嫚) is from the Portuguese Irmao meaning Brother. The term "Father" and "Brother" are Catholic Designations in the Monastic Orders.

14 Goga (吳我) in the Japanese text.

more send them costly presents of Gold, Silver, Silk and Cotton stuffs they will certainly come."

So Goga was sent the second time, with a present of various precious things.

Now after Urugan had sent back the messenger, he said to Furaten: "The Emperor of Namban sent Goga to call me to his capital, that he might send me to Japan to spread abroad our religion, but I think it is only a scheme of the Emperor who is profoundly avaricious, to gain the hearts of the people. On examining the N.E. signs of the horoscope, I see they are uncommonly pure, so that it would be impossible to adapt my arts to them. I therefore decline going."

Furaten, hearing, said: "You have done right, and how often soever he may send for you, don't go." They went together into their mountain cave.

Now General Goga came the second time, bearing various presents to the cave of Wengan[15] "My great king," said he, "Has sent me with the most pressing order for you to come. These are the presents he has sent your Reverence." So saying, he brought out the presents and spread them out before Urugan. Urugan, seeing them, said: "I am a retired hermit dwelling amongst the mountains; it is not proper for me to lay eyes upon such things as these." So saying, he vanished, and Goga, finding it impossible to do anything, again returned to the capital, and reported the matter. The Emperor said: "Truly he is a sage, let General Goki now go himself."

So the father and son went together, in great state, to the mountains, and urging the strongest reasons, said to Urugan: "Every thing below the heavens, whether high or low belong to the Emperor; whether right or wrong you should obey the Emperor's orders; if you do not, you cannot any longer dwell in these mountains. Urugan after a short silence

15 Wengan, *i.e.* the cave of Urugan according to the Japanese text.

said: "Well, I will obey the Emperor's commands and come, but I have a companion in this mountain, from whom I ought to take leave; please wait a short time." He disappeared, they knew not where. General Goki and his son thought it probable that he was deceiving them, but complied with his request and waited.

Urugan went to Furaten and said: "I have thrice declined going, but the General of the left has come himself and is so urgent that I shall have to comply with the Emperor's command and go with him. It may be it will turn out as it did in deluding the people of China.[16] I will cross over to Japan and see what the prospects are, but I do not think I will succeed in Japan as I did in China; but if affairs turn out well, I will send you a letter, and then you can come to my assistance and thus accomplish the Emperor's wishes." So saying, he took leave of Furaten, and returned to the place where General Goki and his son were waiting for him. They were greatly rejoiced, and causing him to ride in a norimon which they had prepared, they returned to the capital of Namban.

The Emperor, exceedingly rejoiced, said to Urugan: "Reverend Sir, I have sent for you in order to send you to Japan to spread abroad the religion of the Padre, and bring the Japanese into obedience; after you have so done, it is my intention, with a large army, to conquer Japan and annex it to my dominion. Although it is a small country, it is a Kingdom of the Gods, and, for the most part, a country of benevolence and justice, so you will find it hard to bring it into obedience as much as you possibly can; therefore, win them with your miraculous powers; besides, you must take presents with you."

It was decided that he would take seven kinds of rare and valuable things with him. The first was a telescope, by which objects could be seen with one eye at a distance of twenty-five miles; the second was a miscrocope for looking at objects as

---

16 China; see note page 8.

small as a poppy-seed[17]; the third was a tiger's skin; the fourth was an air-gun, which could kill at a distance of 450 feet; the fifth was 100 lbs. of sandal-wood; the sixth was a mosquito net, twelve feet square, which when folded could be put into a box three-quarters of an inch square; the seventh was a rosary called Kondats,[18] made of the purple gold of Namba, having 42 beads. These, besides many other curios, were given to Urugan.

After some days, he set sail in a ship of Namban, and having passed one year and a half at sea, at length arrived at Nagasaki, in the provence of Hizen[19]. Purposely dressed up in his foreign costume to attract attention, he walked about from place to place, visiting the Buddhist and Shinto temples. Being a strange looking man, and of barbarous appearance, people regarded him as a wonder, and flocked to see him, so that it was soon rumoured at Miako that a strange looking foreigner had arrived at Nagasaki.

It may be well to state here that when the Shiogun Nobu-Tera,[20] was slain by Miyoshi, his younger brother Yoshi-Aki, who was then a priest in the monastery of Ichi-jo-in[21] in

---

17 According to the Japanese text "poppy-seed" should read "芥子 Karashi" meaning mustard-seed.

18 Kondats. In the Japanese text, 權立, Gondatsu, a corruption from either the Spanish "Cuentas" or Portuguese "Contos"; even to-day the Rosary is known as "Kondatsu". It is equivalent to the English term "telling beads", Cuentas or Contos meaning Numbers or Counts.

19 Kagoshima was the place where Christianity was first introduced but since Nagasaki in Hizen became later the centre of Christian work and trade, it is not surprising that tradition has assigned the honour to that town.

20 Nobuteru. Here there seems to be an error in the translation. According to the original it should be Yoshiteru, the 14th Shogun of the Ashikaga Line, who was slain by Miyoshi, his Minister, in 1565. He was succeeded by Yoshiaki who gained his rank by the support of Nobunaga.

21 Ichijoin, a temple, which existed until the Meiji Restoration period of 1868.

Nanto,[22] left the priesthood, and fled into the province of Goshiu; and Odakadzan-no-tszke-Taira-no-Nobu-naga,[23] the Lord of the Castle of Adzchi in Goshiu,[24] proclaimed him Shiogun. The Emperor Ogimachi, highly approving of this, allowed Nobunaga to come to his palace, so that his power was like that of the dragon when it gets in a cloud, and the five Southern provinces bent to him, like the trees and grass bending to the wind. Receiving the appointment of K'wan-rei-shoku,[25] he lived at the castle of Adzchi. Now hearing, through those about him, of the fact of a strange looking foreigner having arrived at Nagasaki, he felt greatly desirous of seeing him, so he ordered Szge-no-yaku-uye-mon[26] Naga-Hide, one of his ministers, to send and bring him to Kioto. Naga-Hide replied, that "Nagasaki being in the territory belonging to Riu-zo-ji-Taka-shige,[27] who was not one of his friends, he was not at liberty to do so." Nobu-naga replied "that was very true," and told him to send one of the officers of Yoshiaki with the story that the Shiogun wanted him. So, instructing a person by the name of Sasaraya-gen-nay[28] in the matter, and giving out that he was confined to the desire of Yoshi-aki, delivered a false message and a letter to Taka-shige, who, when

---

22 Nanto, the Southern Capital or Nara. The word is also sometimes used to denote the Kofukuji Temple at Nara.

23 Oda Kazusa-no-suke Taira-no-Nobunaga, *i.e.* Oda Nobunaga, was descended from the Taira Family who held power from 1167 to 1185; he was once Governor of Kazusa. Oda is the family name. Kazusa-no-suke means Governor of Kazusa, Taira-no means that he was descended from the Taira Family, and Nobunaga is his personal name.

24 Azuchi; Goshiu *i.e.* (安土：江州) Goshu or Omi-no-kuni.

25 Kwanryoshoku (管領職) Vice-Shogun or Chief Assistant of the Shogun or Military Ruler.

26 Suganoya Kuyemon (菅谷九右衛門).

27 Riuzoji Takashige or Takanobu; he was Daimyo of Saga 1553 to 1569, when he was killed in battle against Shimazu Yoshihiro of Satsuma. Riuzoji was continually at war with his Christian neighbours the Daimyos or Feudal Lords of Omura and Arima.

28 Saburiya Gennai (左分利谷源内).

he had reverently opened and read it, sent the man of Namban in a light norimon, accompanied by two interpreters and some of his own servants, to go up to Miako. But Nobu-naga, not intending from the first that he should go to Miako, sent messengers to meet him on the way at To-ji-yatsz-dzka[29] and Toba-nairate,[30] and brought him straight to Adzchi. When Taka-shige heard of this he gnashed his teeth, saying, " it was trick of that perfidious villain Nobu-naga."

Now, about this time there was a strange event, for on the 24th day of the 8th month of 11th year of the period called Yenroku,[31] 66 venerable fine trees which stood before a Shinto temple in the province of Senchu, called Szmiyashi,[32] were up-rooted by an earthquake and fell. The priest of the temple Setsz-no-kami[33] reported the matter to the Emperor Ogimachi. The Emperor wondered, saying : " That is just the number of provinces in this Empire. What kind of an omen can it be ?" and had prayers offered up at all the Buddhist and Shinto temples in the five provinces about Miyako. Afterwards, in reflecting about it, he thought it must have been an omen of the coming of the Padre to subjugate Japan to the Kingdom of Namban, for the arrival of the Padre at Miyako was just ten days after the falling of the pine trees.

To resume our story, the foreigner having arrived at the castle of Adzchi, Nobunaga sent word to him to rest in a Buddhist temple called Miyohoji,[34] belonging to the sect of Nichiren.[35] After entertaining him handsomely for three days, he

---

29 Toji Yotsuzuka (東寺四塚).

30 Toba Nawate (鳥羽繩手).

31 Yenroku, *i.e.* Eiroku (永祿) A.D. 1558 to A.D. 1570.

32 Sumiyoshi, near Osaka ; Senshu, *i.e.* Izumi-no-kuni (和泉國).

33 Settsu-no-Kami (攝津守), Governor of Settsu ; according to the Japanese text the Governor was Kunitoyo, who was then High Priest at the Sumiyoshi Shrine (住吉神社).

34 Myohoji (妙法寺).

35 Nichiren (日蓮).

admitted him to an audience on the 6th day of the 9th month. Seated upon his throne, his family on his left, and his high ministers Hashiba-Chikuzen-no-kami, Niwa-go-ro-zaemon, and Szge-no-yakuemon, on his right,[36] he was introduced by Hasegawa-take-maru.[37] The presents were placed on a vermillion lacquered stand, and the most celebrated perfume was made to give forth its fragrance. Urugan stood at the foot of the steps, while Nobunaga looked at him from a distance. Urugan was different from ordinary men ; he was more than 9 feet high,[38] head small, colour red, eyes round, teeth like those of horses and whiter than snow, his hair and beard of a rat colour, his age appeared to be about fifty, his coat appeared to be made of cotton ; it was short in the skirts, with long sleeves, and buttoned on the right side ; on his head he wore a vulgar-looking bonnet, in his bosom he carried a perfume which diffused its odours all around. His mode of salutation was by putting his feet together, placing his hand on his breast, and bowing low. Nobunaga inquired of him, through Inoszke,[39] the interpreter, " for what reason he had come to this country from Namban ?" He replied : " In order to publish religion." "What is your name?" He replied: "Padre Urugan." Nobunaga, hearing, said: "As to the matter of your publishing religion, it will be, in my opinion, very difficult ; but we will

---

36 Hashiba Chikuzen-no-Kami (羽柴筑前守). The same as Toyotomi Hideyoshi; before he rose to power Hideyoshi used the name Hashiba.
Niwa Gorozaemon (丹羽五郎左衛門). Possibly identical with Niwa Nagahide, Daimyo of Sawayama, who was entrusted by Nobunaga with the building of Azuchi Castle.
Suganoya Kuyemon, see page 14.

37 Hasegawa Takemaru (長谷川竹丸) or Hasegawa Chikurando (長谷川竹蘭堂). There was a Hasegawa at the Court of Hideyoshi who introduced the Franciscans from Manila in 1593.

38 There was a tradition that Priests were all tall, owing to the great height of Valignani, the Jesuit, who visited Nobunaga on several occasions at Azuchi.

39 Inoko Hyosuke (猪子兵助).

think more about this by and by." He then ordered one of his ministers to make him a present of many rare things.

Now, after this, Nobunaga assembled all his ministers, together with the Buddhist priests, the learned men, (*lit.* Confucionists) and physicians to his castle of Adzchi, and said: "In respect of the foreigner who has now come for the purpose of publishing religion, it is difficult for me alone to decide; let each one of you freely express his opinion for or against allowing him to carry out his desire." When the whole assembly was silent, and no one seemed disposed to reply, the great Confucionist Bunki-yoinho Kiyo Dosen,[40] advancing, said:

"It appears to me that man of Namban is a very vulgar looking fellow, and not the kind of man to teach religion. The Shinto religion, Confucianism, and Buddhism prevail, and are flourishing. I think it would be quite useless for him to teach a new religion; your Majesty had better immediately order him to return to his own country." Nobunaga reflecting for a short time, and feeling in his heart that, right or wrong, he would like him to spread abroad religion, said: "What Dosen has said seems to be in one view proper enough, and should not be obstinately rejected; but as to the religions prevalent in this country, we find that they have all been brought from foreign countries, for about a thousand years after the death of Shaka, Mato[41] brought the Buddhist sacred books to China on a white horse, and afterwards gave them to Kenso,[42] the second Emperor of the Kan Dynasty, who honoured him,

---

40 Bunkyoin Dosen (文敬院道仙); presumably the same as Manase Dosan, who was famous about this time as a Buddhist scholar and sage; he became Court Physician to Hideyoshi and was eventually converted to Christianity by Father Figueiredo.

41 Mato (摩騰): Matanga.

42 Kenso (顯宗); the full title of this Emperor was Kenso Komei Kotei (顯宗孝明皇帝) A.D. 58–75. Kan is the Japanese pronounciation of Han.

and invited him to the temple of Koroji.[43] Finally, Buddhism spread through the 400 and more provinces of the Empire. Again, in the reign of Kinmei,[44] the 30th Emperor of Japan, (A. D. 552) Buddhism was brought to this country from Chorea ; it has spread and become flourishing ; and now also it is impossible for us to know how excellent the religion may be which the Padre wishes to propagate, wherefore my mind is made up to allow him to spread it abroad as much as he pleases. Let each one of you understand this." The assembly was then dismissed.

After this, Nobunaga ordered Szge-no-ya-kuemon[45] to get a flat ot ground, 864 feet square, in the fourth ward of Miyako called Bomon,[46] to bring large stones from the North[47] Mountain, for building a wall around it ; and regardless of the cost, to build a church of seven halls to be called after the name of the year, Yenrokuji.[48] But when the Buddhists of the Yensan[49] Monastery heard of it, they consulted together and said : " No other temple but our Yenriyakuji has ever been called after the name of the year. In the reign of Hei-sho,[50] the

---

43 Koroji (鴻臚寺) ; this was not a Buddhist Temple but it was a special office or department for receiving distinguished guests. The character "寺" used to mean Department.

44 Kinmei Tenno (欽明天皇) A.D. 540–571.

45 Suganoya Kuyemon, see page 14.

46 Nambanji, or the first Christian Church in Kyoto, was built in 1568 near the gate called Shijo Bōmon (四條坊門) ; the Church was destroyed in 1588 after Hideyoshi issued his first Anti-Christian Edict. The Church Bell was taken to Myoshinji Temple whence in in 1906 it was removed to Ueno Museum in Tokyo.

47 Kitayama (北山) ; the hills to the north of Kyoto.

48 Yeirokuji (永祿寺).

49 Yeizan (叡山) ; Hiyeisan, the group of Monasteries on the hills outside Kyoto.

50 Heisho (平城) *i.e.* Heijo Tenno (平城天皇), also known to history as the Nara-no-Mikado.

51st Emperor, and in the second year of the era called Dai-do,[51] a temple was built in the province of Yamato,[52] on the hill Kata-o, which was called Dai-doji after the name of the year, but this monastery would not permit it, and the sign-board having the above name inscribed on it was broken to pieces; this is a sure precedent, and why should Nobunaga, now, call this temple Yenroku? It is indeed throwing contempt upon the royal throne of this whole Empire; there is no reason why it should be allowed." In this judgment they were all unanimous. Over three hundred of them, clad in armour under their priestly robes, went in procession to the palace and handed up a written complaint; others, in a great crowd, carried the sacred shrine of the god, and with much noise and tumult went to complain, alarming the Mikado greatly. The Mikado immediately assembled his high council, and sent Hiromaki,[53] as a messenger to Nobunaga, saying: " I am glad that, on account of the respect you have for Buddhism, you are now building a temple at Miyako; but as no temple must be called by the name of the year except Yenriyakuji,[54] I feel greatly troubled on account of the complaint of the priests. You will therefore at once change the name of the temple."

Nobunaga was much displeased, but as it was an Imperial command, he could not disobey, and accordingly changed the name into Nambanji.[55] Nobunaga's resentment was deep, as he had built the temple himself. He said to Urugan: " As your bigoted opponents are many and you are alone, you will find it difficult to propagate your religion; you had better send to Namban and call some priests to help you, and spread abroad religion as widely as possible." At the same time he gave him

51 Daido (大同), A.D. 806–809.

52 Yamato-no-kuni of Nara Prefecture (奈良縣大和國).

53 Kazanin Chunagon Hiromasa Kyo (花山院中納言廣政卿).

54 Yenriyakuji (延暦寺), the temple on Mount Hiei.

55 Nambanji (南蠻寺).

land in the province of Goshu[56] that would yield a revenue of 500 K'was[57] (about 80 Riyo). Urugan, smiling, did as he was told, and sent a letter to the King of Namban in order to call Padre Furaten, as he had before promised. The letter was as follows: "All things are favourable in Japan; through the orders of Nobunaga I am prospering greatly in propagating religion as I wish. Therefore call Furaten, and send him to Japan as quickly as possible." Besides this he wrote a letter to Furaten. The King was greatly rejoiced, and quickly sent for Furaten and told him to go at once to Japan and assist Urugan in accomplishing his great object. Furaten replied "that Japan could not be brought into subjection by religious arts merely." The King asked: "What plan then would you adopt"? Furaten replied: "Most men are afflicted with either poverty or disease; if I went to Japan I would aid the poor by giving them gold and silver, and the sick I would supply with medicine,[58] and thus deliver them from poverty and disease; explaining the three words—the past, present and future—and convincing them by various miracles; then, with the mirror of the three worlds[59] which I possess, I would lead them as I did the Chinese, and so bring Japan for the most part into submission, and then your Majesty can take such measures as you think best." The King was greatly rejoiced, and consulting with Gen. Goki,[60] he got ready gold and silver and many kinds of medicines. Now, in a place called Nambikoto,[61] there was some wonderful and celebrated physicians who had received their education in India. Two of these, one called Gerido, the

56 Goshu (江州), Omi-no-kuni of Shiga Prefecture.

57 Kwasi, *i.e.* Kwan (8¼ lbs.); Riyo *i.e.* Ryo (兩).

58 The early missionaries founded several hospitals, notably the Kiusaiin (救濟院) and the Koshitsu-in (痼疾院) at Funai, Bungo, by Luis Almeida; the Misericordia and Hospicio de Santiago at Nagasaki and the Bethlehem Convent at Osaka. At Ibukiyama in Omi they had a medicinal farm or college.

59 Mirror of the Three Worlds *i.e.* the past, present and future worlds.

60 Goki (吳輝).

61 Nambikoto (南ビコドウ) in the Japanese text.

other Yois, both Romans,[62] were associated with Furaten and sent to Japan, and their expenses defrayed by the taxes received from fifteen of the Eastern provinces.

Now, after the lapse of many days, they arrived near Nagasaki, in the province of Hizen, but Furaten, examining the heavenly conjunctions, said: "If the ship stops at Nagasaki some calamity will befall us; if we put into a Northern province all will be well." Now this he said because he feared that Tagashige,[63] the Prince of Hizen, would certainly interfere with him, on account of the deception practiced on him before by Nobunaga, in getting Urugan to his castle at Adzchi, and not because of any signs he saw in the heavens. Therefore, passing by Nagasaki and Yszshima,[64] they landed on the island of Ike.[65] The Prince of this country hearing of it, and fearing that if he allowed the foreigners to enter Japan without restraint some trouble might grow out of it, would not let them land until he had examined into it. But an interpreter telling him that Nobunaga had sent for these men from Namban, and showing him letters that had been written to Nobunaga and Urugan, through fear of the power of Nobunaga, he suffered them to land. From there they sailed in a Japanese ship and landed at Ohama in the province of Osa;[66] from thence they went to the Namban monastery, where they met Urugan. They were all greatly rejoiced in meeting, and passed the time in talking. After resting four or five days they went

---

62 Romans *i.e.* Irmaos, in Portuguese meaning Brothers.

Gerido—"Gerikori" (ゲリコリ) in the Japanese text—may be identical with Figueiredo, a Jesuit who was in Japan in 1564 and later converted Manase Dosan.

Yois—Yariisu Iruman in the Japanese text—may possibly refer to either Luis Almeida or Lawrence, a Japanese Brother much favoured by Hideyoshi.

63 Riuzoji Takashige or Takanobu (龍造寺高重).

64 Tsushima (對馬).

65 Iki, an island off Kyushiu, the southern island of Japan.

66 Obama (小濱); Osa (若狹) *i.e.* Wakasa of Fukui Prefecture.

to Adzchi, and stopped as before in the temple of Miyohoji.[67] The three men afterwards went to the castle and were introduced to Nobunaga. The ceremonies were the same as on the previous occasion, when Urugan was received. The presents were of five kinds, *viz*, a ruby censer, one ball of musk, an agate cane, ten tiger skins and fifty pieces of woollen cloth of different colours. Furaten was ten feet-and-a-half in height, his hair and beard were yellow, and his dress the same as Urugan. After being handsomely entertained, they took leave of Nobunaga and returned to the monastery of Namban.

After these things the Padre and Romans[68] put their wits together and devised various plans. Furaten, in order to aid the sick, having brought a large quantity of medicinal plants, requested Nobunaga to give him a plot of ground, where he might plant the seed. A suitable place was found in Ibukiyama, in the province of Omi,[69] and a plantation of two miles square was laid out for this purpose.

The monastery of Namban became daily more grand, adorned with the richest ornaments of gold and precious stones, and brocade hangings. The perfume of the sweetest incense penetrated the nostrils of persons passing along outside of the gate. Not only the people of the five provinces around Miyako[70] but those from the Island of Shikoku, and from the eastern and western provinces, came in great numbers to Miyako, to see the temple of Namban. Every day persons were sent to hunt up and bring the outcasts and beggars who slept under the bridges, the incurable sick left to die in the hills and moors, besides the very sick and hard to cure, from

---

67 Myohoji (妙法寺).

68 Brothers.

69 Ibukiyama (伊吹山); Omi, the same as Goshu in Shiga Prefecture. At Ibukiyama the Portuguese maintained a medicinal herb farm.

70 Gokinai (五畿内) namely Yamato, Yamashiro, Kawachi, Settsu and Izumi.

every place. To the poor money was given, and out of every ten that the Romans prescribed for, eight or nine were restored to health. Clothing was also given them ; those who were yesterday wearing rags, to-day were wrapped in silk. The number of those who blessed their beneficence could not be counted.

The two Romans would say to these persons thus : " The reason we came so far to Japan was at the command of the King of Namban. The country of Namban has 42 provinces, and is a hundred times larger than Japan, but being the real King of Heaven, and worshipping Jesus, there are no severely sick persons in it ; and because the King rules his people with kindness, the country is prosperous and rich. It is entirely owing to the benevolence of the King, that we are sent to a country in which the religion of Jesus has not yet been propagated ; we come to help the sick and afflicted—and the two Padres to teach religion. As this religion has not yet been spread in Japan, the poor and sick people abound ; consequently, thieves and dissolute persons are numerous. If in this world we commit sin, we cannot attain to eternal life in the next. All this comes from not worshipping Jesus. Now let us show what you will be in the next world." So saying, they brought out the Mirror of the Three Worlds, and told them to look into it, one after the other. Some appeared to have the head of a cow, some with a horse's face, and others with shapes of various kinds of birds. " Alas ! how lamentable will be our condition in the next world," they all said, crying in sorrow. Then the two Romans said : " If you would have your sins blotted out, you must obey the religion of the God of Heaven. First learn this prayer." So saying, they gave them the Rosary called Kondatsz,[71] having 42 beads, and repeated this prayer : " Shigo shoten paparaiso usen

71 Gondatsz—Gondatsu in the Japanese text (権立). See page 13.

szmaro."[72] They told them every time they said this prayer they must tell one of the beads of the Rosary, and continue saying it for seven days, so their sins would be blotted out without any doubt ; then they should show themselves to the head Padre of the monastery and receive the great conversion, and their going to the good place in the next world would be perfectly sure. There, too, they would be allowed to worship Jesus. When he said these things they were all greatly rejoiced, and as they were instructed, confined themselves to the house, saying over the prayer and telling the Rosary. After the seven days were accomplished, under the guidance of the Romans, they went to the dwelling place of the Padre. This shone and glittered with golden ornaments, and was filled with the odour of the most fragrant perfume ; they could hardly believe it belonged to this world. The two Padres, in red and golden robes, sat benignantly, so that they doubted whether they might not be the living body of God Himself. Then the Roman said to them : " You have now been made to perform that which was painful and difficult ; your diseases are cured ; for seven days you have particularly observed these religious duties. Now behold the blessed results." So they caused them to look into the mirror they had seen before, and lo ! their appearance had completely changed, their skin had become of the colour of the finest gold, and their countenances so beautiful that without thinking, they exclaimed, " Oh ! how glorious " and shed tears of admiration. The Padre then said to them : " If such are the wonderful changes from performing these religious duties for the short space of seven days only, what shall be said of constant faith ? That you would then become like God Himself in the future state there can be no doubt. If, in addition,

72 The Japanese text of this prayer is Shigo Shoten Haraiso Uzen Shumaro (死後生天波羅夷僧有善主磨呂). Shigo, after death ; Shoten is born in Heaven ; Haraiso, Paradise ; Uzen, will be good ; Shumaro, important or chiet person. The meaning, therefore, seems to be "After death let me be born in a Heavenly Paradise and remain there a chief person" or, freely, "After death bring us to Heavenly Paradise".

you altogether worship Jesus and the King of Heaven ; although you should be at once broken on the wheel, or cut to pieces, in the future world you would certainly be saved by the power of Jesus, whom you should worship in faith." So saying, he brought out a thing called a cross, (*Jap.* Kurus) ; this was made of gold, the upper part was two inches square, with a handle two feet long, and on both sides full of sharp points like a radish grater ; them having made then, bare their bodies, with this cross he scraped and tore their backs.[73] The pain was excessive and the blood flowed. He anointed their right and left hands with the blood and made them join them together. "The Honourable Founder of this Christianity, called Jesus, also called Lord of Heaven, is the Creator of all things, of heaven and earth, sun, moon, animals, trees, and grass ; Who treats all alike as His children. Still, in these last times, people, through their wicked hearts and corrupt lusts, oppose the Heart of Jesus, and do not reverence Him. Let a man be as wicked as he may, yet if he loves Jesus, he will be happy in Paradise, which is Heaven, where every thing will be according to his mind ; of this there can be no doubt. Now, let all of you draw near to the secret chamber where Jesus is worshipped, and bow down." So saying, he opened a door, and lo ! an image of Jesus, fearfully represented, hanging upon a cross. "This," he said, "is the illustrious Founder of our religion ; this figure is a representation of the difficult and painful sufferings he endured in former ages, in order to give happiness to those who believe in the King of Heaven." They all burst into a back chamber called the Tai-men,[74] to worship

---

73 This part seems to refer to the traditions of flagellation which was much practiced in Japan by converts. One or two "disciplines" preserved by the Christians are to be seen in the Museum at Urakami Cathedral, Nagasaki.

74 Taimen-no-ma (對面の間).

the picture of Taishakuten[75]. This was the figure of a beautiful woman, having a cap of pearls upon her head, clothed in gorgeous robes, and holding in her bosom a child with the breast in its mouth. The Padre said: "This is a tradition of our religion, and is a representation of the tender love of the King of Heaven to such simple ones as you, which is like a mother holding her child in her bosom and giving it suck; quick, bow down," he said, and they joined their bloody hands together: and repeating the prayer of "After death bring us to heaven," bowed down and worshipped.

Now after this, through the persuasions of the people, a great many persons connected themselves with this sect. From amongst the above-mentioned sick persons there were three, who were particularly intelligent and clever, that were retained for the services of the monastery. One of them whose name was Yeshun,[76] was a Buddhist priest of the Sen sect[77] from the province of Kaga[78]. Being a leper, disgusting to look at, with whom no one would associate, he left his native province, and becoming a beggar and an outcast, wandered to Miako. Here, falling down, he was unable to rise, and when life was almost extinguished, he was brought to the temple of Namban, and by the medical skill of the Romans, was gradully restored to health and to his original appearance; on this account he joined this sect, and his name changed to

---

75 Taishakuten (帝釋天). Tai "帝" is the Chinese translation of the Sanskrit "Indra," meaning Lord or King; Shaku "釋" is the Chinese for "Sakra" meaning Mighty; and Ten "天" is the Chinese of the Sanskrit "Deva".

The use of this term here is curious because the God described is a Female God and Taishakuten could never have been female; it is more probable that the reference is to Komochi Kwannon (子持觀音). *i.e.* Avalokitesvara, the Goddess of Mercy, whose statue was used by the Christians, after the persecution, for the purpose of worship as Mary, the Mother of Jesus.

76 Yeshun (慧春).

77 Zenshu (禪宗).

78 Kaga-no-kuni (加賀國) in Ishikawa Prefecture.

Babiman.[79] Another was called Yaszzayemon,[80] a merchant from the province of Senshu, and well known, but neglecting his business, being fond of pleasure and dissolute, he ruined himself by his profligacy; so having squandered all his property, and not being able to find a place to live in, he became a beggar and an outcast. He was diseased, and wandered about here and there, keeping himself alive by eating the scraps that people left. The third person was a farmer from the province of Idzmi,[81] hamlet of Kurota,[82] by the name of Zengoro. This man had formerly been a rich man, but being profligate and fond of gambling, he gradually became a low fellow. Being diseased and of digusting appearance, avoided by others, having neither a home nor character, he at last came to Miako, and frequented the neighbourhood of the East Temple.[83] One day, being under the portico of this temple, he and his fellow countryman Yaszzayemon laid eyes on each other. They were both ashamed, but approaching, they talked of old times, and deplored the miserable end to which they had come. After some time had elapsed, both of these men were cured of their disease at Nambanji. They were clothed, filled with good food, and their names changed, Yaszzayemon being called Goszmo[84] while Zengoro was called Junmon.[85] The above three men made their home together in Nambanji.

The two Padres frequently taught these men to repeat the Darani (Ave Maria) and to perform various miracles, such as to change a handkerchief into a horse, to make a bird out

---

79 Baian (梅庵); possibly John, as other Japanese manuscripts refer to a "Haiyan," obviously a corruption of John. All converts received a Christian baptismal name.

80 Yasuzayemon (安左衛門); in the Japanese text he is described as a dealer in textiles in the country of Izumi.

81 Idzmi, *i.e.* Izumi (和泉).

82 Kuromura (黒村) in the Japanese text.

83 Toji (東寺) in Kyoto.

84 Gozsmo, *i.e.* Cosmo.

85 Junmon (シユモン) Shumon, *i.e.* Simon.

of dust, to make a withered tree blossom, to turn clods of earth into pearls, to sit upon the air, descend into the earth, to cause clouds to rise, and make it rain or snow. But two of them, Goszmo and Junmon, after this sect was broken and destroyed, lived in the border of the province of Senshu, where they wrought miracles. Hideyoshi called them to his castle at Fushimi, and being convicted of working miracles, they were punished with death.

Besides these three men, persons who had been cured of their diseases were sent out, in the garb of merchants, not only around Miako, but to all the neighbouring provinces, using every means to persuade the people, and preaching everywhere about the love and kindness to be found at Nambanji "where," said they, "there are two celebrated physicians called Romans, both surgeon and physician, who treat every form of disease, even the most incurable, without failing to cure in a single instance, and who will not receive one cash in remuneration, even if they should be burnt for it. Moreover, they supply their patients with food, and to those that are poor, who have wives and children remaining at home, they give money; truly their compassion is great. This must be the religion in which a person at once becomes divine quickly; change your religion and become the followers of Jesus." By circulating such persuasions, great numbers of the grievously poor, sick and afflicted, joined this sect; and when it became gradually circulated from one to another, that food was provided for the sick, and also the wants of their wives, children, and all the members of their families, how numerous soever they might be, were cared for, even those who were but a little sick came and joined them. Thus this religion day by day grew and prospered, so that not only the common people of the towns and the farmers, but great numbers of the military class and nobility became its followers. Now, in order to bring Japan into subjection to Namban, and to supply funds for this purpose, ships came from Namban yearly, bringing the revenue of fifteen of the provinces. The Padres sent back a register of the number of persons who joined them yearly to the King—so many hundreds this year, so many thousands this year, and of the success of their stratagem to subjugate the country without the use of military weapons.

Nobunaga, hearing the reports of the extraordinary doings of this sect, in his heart repented of what he had done, as it constantly became more and more numerous. Fearing that it might be a source of trouble in the future, he assembled his Ministers and said:

" There are many marvellous stories about the Temple of Namban that I built, especially of their giving money to those persons who join them. Now as respects the Buddhist, it is a rule that every one shall make some offering to the temple if it be only a roll of paper,[86] or half a Zeni;[87] but, on the contrary, that alms should be given out from the monastery makes this sect look very suspicious. I am now, at least, heartily sorry that I did not follow the advice that Dozen gave at first. If I let it alone, it is impossible to say how great an evil it may become. Let each of you give his opinion, whether I had not better destroy this sect, and send the Padres home to their own country."

Mayeda and Geni,[88] sitting together, boldly advanced and said:

" As to Nambanji and the subject of destroying it, we think your Majesty has delayed it too long. For already has the religion spread, not only over Miako, but all the neighbouring provinces of the nobles, the military class, your

---

86 One sheet of paper in the Japanese text (一紙).

87 Sen (錢).

88 "Mayeda and Geni sitting together". This seems to be a mistranslation as the Japanese text is " Mayeda Tokuzenin Geni Hoin (前田德善院玄意法印) happened to be there". Mayeda Geni was Minister of Worship and Governor of Kyoto under Hideyoshi. He was very friendly towards the Christians and did his best to save them.

Majesty's own retainers,—and even of this assembly, many honour the sect, and have joined the religion of Jesus. If you determine to destroy it at once, it is impossible to say how great the disturbance and revolt it might occasion. Your Majesty had better wait until a more favourable time."

Nobunaga, assenting to the truth of this, said: "As I am so ignorant, whenever you have a suitable plan, tell it without hesitation." The assembly was then dismissed.

Soon after this it was reported to Nobunaga by express that Araki Settsz-no-kami[89] had rebelled, and was about to make war on him. When Nobunaga heard it, he could not believe this was possible of one of his most meritorious generals, and thinking it must be a mistake sent Akechi Hiyoga-no-kami[90] to ascertain the truth. As there remained no doubt about the truth of the rebellion, orders were given to suppress it, when it was reported that Takayama[91] had also joined the rebels. Nobunaga said that "he had heard that Takayama was one of the sect of Jesus; now this sect professes to make it its principal study to have no connection with unrighteousness, but here is Takayama making common cause with rebellion. I will therefore destroy this sect." The

---

89 Araki Settsu-no-Kami Murashige; *i.e.* Araki, family name; Settsu-no-kami, Governor of Settsu; Murashige, personal name.

90 Akechi Hyuga-no-Kami (明智日向守).

91 Takayama Ukon Shogen (高山左近將監). Takayama family name; Ukon Shogen a military office of very high rank under the Shogun in ancient times.

Don Justo Takayama, as known to the missionaries, is one of the most notable figures of Christianity in Japan in the 16th and 17th centuries. Other Daimyos, like Otomo Yoshishige, Konishi Yukinaga, and Omura Sumitada were perhaps more powerful and suffered as much for their Faith but they never threatened to wield so much influence in the land as Takayama. The proof of this is that Hideyoshi obviously feared the abilities of Takayama else he would never have bothered to turn him out of his small fiefs, first at Takatsuki, and later at Akashi. The fears of Hideyoshi were evidently shared by Iyeyasu Tokugawa, his successor, who banished Don Justo to Manila, where he died in 1617.

Padres were called, and when this intention was made known to them, they were astounded. Now Sakuma,[92] Kunaikujo and Otezden (three of Nobunaga's principal generals) who also belonged to this sect, went to the castle of Takayama[93] and informed him of the intention of Nobunaga, and persuaded him to submit to reason and return to his allegiance, and to give hostages to Nobunaga to this effect. On this account the destruction of the monastery of Namban was again put off.

Now, after this the country was gradually restored to tranquility, and Nobunaga became Shogun over the whole empire. During his whole reign the Christain Padres propagated their religion as much as they pleased ; but the country being again thrown into confusion, Nobunaga at last, in the 10th year, 6th month and 2nd day of the era called Tensho[94] in the rebellion of Akechimits-hide,[95] was killed in Honji[96] in Kiyoto.[96a] Akechi-mits-hide was also slain by Hideyoshi, and Hideyoshi became Shogun who grasping the four seas, tranquilized the whole empire. Thus the Namban monastery and the Christian religion flourished from the 11th year of the era called Yenroku,[97] until the 13th year of the era called Tensho, which was 18 years. It was finally destroyed by Hideyoshi.

Now while this sect was most flourishing, owing to distributing money daily without distinction, to priests and

---

92 Sakuma Uyemon (佐久間右衛門); he was a famous general under Nobunaga who gave him the Province of Kaga after its conquest from the Monto Sect of Buddhist priests ; here Takayama took refuge after being defiefed by Hideyoshi.
Kunai Kyo Hoin (宮内卿法印).
Otsu Denjuro (大津傳十郎).

93 The Japanese text reads "Castle of Takatsuki", the residence of Takayama.

94 Tensho (天正) A.D. 1573–1591.

95 Akechi Mitsuhide (明智光秀).

96 Honnoji (本能寺).

96a At the date in question was called Miyako.

97 Yeiroku (永綠) A.D. 1558–1569.

citizens, men and women, not only in the five provinces about Miyako, but along the seven great highways,[98] there were monasteries erected, and again monasteries branching out from these, so that the sect became widely extended. Hideyoshi at this time was living in the Castle Yodo.[99] It was his constant opinion that the sect was a suspicious one. The Padres saw that Hideyoshi, so unlike Nobunaga, had no liking for their religion, so they set themselves to devise some way by which they might influence him in their favour. Now, at this time there was a very skillful carpenter called Nakaihanbei,[100] for whom Hideyoshi had a great liking, and whom he kept always near him. He afterwards promoted him over all the others, changed his name to Shuri,[101] and presented him with a house. Everybody strove to please him. Placing his old mother with a female servant in the house, he himself was always attending to his duty near to Hideyoshi. Now Babiman,[102] who dwelled at the Namban monastery thought no better plan could be devised than to win over this Shuri to join the sect, and so make use of him to influence Hideyoshi; being the head man, all the carpenters of the empire would, of course, follow his example and join the sect.

In the first place he set himself about to devise a plan to induce his mother to join them. So one day, accompanied with a servant handsomely dressed and riding in a norimon, he came about the time of sunset to Kiyoto, and stopped before the house of Shuri. He sent his servant to say to the mother that a priest from the main temple at Kiyoto, having gone to the province Senshu[103] on business, returning, had become

---

98 Seven great high ways *i.e.* Shichido (七道).
99 Yodo in Kyoto Prefecture.
100 Nakai Hanbei (中井半兵衛).
101 Shuri (修理); Shuri tayu (修理大夫), *i.e.* Master Carpenter, an official title.
102 See page 27 and note No. 79.
103 See page 27.

belated; and as the country was in a disturbed state, he was afraid to enter Kiyoto in the night, and seeing this dwelling he prayed for a night's lodging. The old mother believing what he said, although the master of the house was absent, yet as it was an honourable priest who wanted lodging, she could not refuse, and gave him her best guest-chamber to rest in. The old mother went to the door, and gave him a friendly welcome; Babiman acknowledged the favour, and lodged there that night.

At early dawn the next day, expressing his deep obligation for the many kindnesses, he took his departure for Kiyoto. A few days after, a two-sworded man, accompanied by a sandal-bearer and other servants, bearing boxes and trays, came to the house of Shuri, saying: "I am a messenger come from Babiman, Namban Monastery in Kiyoto. Having lately with great trouble entertained him so handsomely, and that a stranger, he wishes you to accept of some expression of his gratitude." So saying, he laid on the table five rolls of brocade, a pound of frankincense, besides other rare things. The old mother, feeling that these things were beyond all proportion too many and valuable, made many excuses, declining; but the messenger, having a clever tongue, at last persuaded her to accept them, and after being politely entertained, returned. After this, Babiman frequently sent presents of silk and sweetmeats, so that the intimacy became quite thick.

The next autumn, hitting upon a time when showers of rain were likely to occur, Babiman, ostensibly to go to Senshu, and purposely leaving Kiyoto late in the day, called at the house of Shuri, to express his thanks for previous politeness.

The old mother thanked him for the presents he had recently made her, and prepared various good things for his entertainment. As the sun was already set, and especially as it looked like rain, she invited him to remain there for the night. As this was just what he wanted, with many thanks for her kindness, he stayed.

In the evening, while conversing, Babiman said: " How strange it is that we should become such good friends; it is all owing to some relation in a previous state. By the way, without knowing what may be your religion, at the present time there is none like the sect to which I belong, Christianity, that can at once make a man a God. If you enter this sect, you would in this world show forth the marks of being divine. Those that belong to other sects cannot even imitate them. Other sects may be compared to brass, mine to fine gold. If you desire to possess this divine nature in this world, change your religion and enter the sect of the Padres, and I will show it to you." Many such arguments did he use and press upon the old mother with great cunning; but she, hearing, said:

" Truly your religion is most wonderful, but from my youth now for more than 60 years, I have only said over the Buddhist prayers, and sought the help of others; indeed this thing, of myself becoming a god in this world, is entirely too much for me even to think of." Babiman replied: " You are mistaken. To become a god in this world, it is not necessary to perform difficult works and painful austerities; if you only worship Jesus and enter this sect, you will become a god. For this reason, more than half of the 60 and more provinces have entered this sect; instead of praying to live in the world to come, it is much better to become like God while in this." Woman as she was, she was much perplexed, and could not decide; so reflecting for a moment she said: " Truly to become divine in this world would be most excellent, but as I am but a woman, I cannot settle my doubts. I have a learned friend in Kiyoto whose teaching of Buddhism I have been accustomed to listen to; I will invite him to come, and after I have heard you discuss the subject with him, I will then change my religion."

Babiman replied, that was very reasonable, and she promised to let him know when her friend came from Kiyoto, so he left early the next morning and returned to Kiyoto.

Now there lived in Kiyoto, in the fourth street[104] near the riding ground,[105] a retired scholar called Hakuo.[106] This man was formerly an inmate of Yeisanji,[107] but having rheumatism in his head which prevented him from shaving off his hair, he could not become a priest, and so had to leave. But following the steps of Yuima[108] (a disciple of Shaka) he lived in a hut nine feet square, and devoted himself to the purifying of his heart. Being informed by the mother of Shuri of the promise she had made to Babiman, Hakuo considered himself very fortunate, for he had always regarded that religion as a wicked one, and had desired all the other sects with one accord to condemn it; but owing to the favour of Nobunaga, and to its being disregarded by Hideyoshi, he had to let it alone. But now he saw a good opportunity offered to discuss and settle its claims, and accordingly fixed a day when he would come. The mother of Shuri was greatly rejoiced, and sending word to Babiman of the appointment, she impatiently waited for the time to come. So on the 13th year of the 9th month Hakuo came to the house of Shuri; soon after Babiman also came. The latter was dressed in a scarlet crape robe, a unique band of Chinese make over his shoulders, and a cap made of cloth, ornamented with flowers on his head, looking very beautiful.

The people of the neighbourhood collected in crowds to

---

104 Fourth Street, Shijo-dori (四條通).

105 Riding Ground, Yanagi-no-baba (柳馬場).

106 Hakuo, a pundit; probably the same as Nichiro Shumon, a favourite of Nobunaga, employed by the Buddhist priests to work against Christianity. Father Froez had an argument on Christianity with him in the presence of Nobunaga, in the course of which Nichiro seized a sword to cut off the head of Brother Lawrence, who was also present, with a view to seeing "a soul living after death." Nichiro was disarmed by Hideyoshi who was in attendance at the time.

107 Hieisan (比叡山).

108 Yuima (維摩). This is an abbreviation of "Yuimakitsu" (維摩詰), a corrupted transliteration of Vimalakrtti, to whom is ascribed the authorship of the Mahayama Sutra "維摩經". (Vimalakrtti-Nirdesa-Sutra).

the house of Shuri to hear the discussion. Babiman, bowing, took his seat. He took a black lacquered box from a trunk and placed it by him on his right side. The salutations ended, Hakuo said:

"What God is it that was the founder of your religion"?

Babiman, without immediately replying, took from the black box several volumes of the Buddhist sacred books, and placing them at his side, said:

"The author of my religion is called Jesus, who, before anything existed between the heavens and the earth, was manifested, (or came into being). When the earth was chaos and the air uninhabited, besides this God there was none else. It was He, who, by His divine power, first created all things, the sun, moon, stars, men, birds, animals, trees and grass. At first the heart of man was righteous, and was in accord with the heart of Jesus. Without asking for it, He enjoyed the happiness of heaven, but in after ages His desires and lusts being strong, He, of Himself became depraved, wherefore compassionating the troubles and calamities of men, gave them this prayer: 'O good Lord Mary, after death bring us to the[109] Heavenly Paradise.' Whoever repeats this prayer, Jesus will save them. The Japanese honour the two Buddhists, Amida and Shaka, and worship Tenshodaijin,[110] but do not know the love of our Jesus. Well, let me ask you what you worship?"

Hakuo, replying, said: "The Niyorai,[111] whom we worship, is what you have just called Amida and Shaka.

Babiman said: "He who is called Amida,[112] was a man who was a priest in a previous state. Shaka[113] was Shitta[114]

---

109 See note page 24.

110 Tenshodaijin (天照大神). Amaterasu Ō Mikami, the Goddess of the Sun.

111 Nyorai (如來); Chinese translation of the Sanskrit Tathagata. One of the honorfic titles given to the Buddhas.

112 Amida (阿彌陀). Amida Buttsu: Sanskrit, Amitabha.

113 Shaka (釋迦) Shaka, *i.e.* Sakya.

114 Shitta (悉多). Sanskrit, Siddhartha.

the eldest son of Jobon,[115] a King of India. Tensho Daijin, was the son of Izanagi and Izanami,[116] the two illustrious children of Heaven. They were all mere men, and it is impossible to conceive that they can save men. Shaka was most disobedient to his parents, for, when 19 years old, he ran away from his home and wandered about in the Tanboku[117] mountains, wearing ragged clothes, spending his whole life in the moors and mountains as a beggar depending upon others, and explaining various laws, so it is said ; also his 16 disciples and 500 followers were just like him, a company of vagabonds, so the Buddhist priests follow his example, receiving alms of others. Those that bestow most alms upon them, they hypocritically flatter, and in order to serve their own religion, they sacrifice the truth. It is because the religion of Jesus is not known in Japan, there is so much poverty and suffering, so many beggars and outcasts wandering in the streets, and so many thieves and bad fellows. Namban, although it is a large empire of 42 provinces, yet because they worship Jesus there, poverty, suffering, severe sickness, beggars and robbers, are quite unknown. This all results from there being no depraved desires; where there is no lust there is no sin, so that even in this world they possess the happiness of heaven. This is the only religion where in this world man becomes a god. Now, if the religion of Shaka and Amida be true, let them punish me, let all of you behold the proof." So saying, he took sacred books of Buddha, and tore them into pieces and trampled on them, then he blew his nose on them and spat on them. Taking his seat he said : " Do you all perceive this, nowithstanding all I have now done, you see I am not smitten with punishment ; the reason is that there is no truth in that religion. Other religions are like brass, mine is the pure gold. Quick—turn

---

115 Jobon (淨飯): Chinese for the Sanskrit Suddhodana.

116 Izanagi (伊弉諾).
Izanami (伊弉冊).

117 Tanboku (檀特): Dandokusan is the Chinese transliteration of the Sanskrit Dantalokagiri ; Sen is (山) Mountain.

away from all other religions and become followers of that religion which in this world will make you a god.

At first, Hakuo replied, once or twice, but as Babiman became so outrageous he looked grave, and said not a word in reply, but sat in silence. The whole assembly sat in mute astonishment (swallowing their spittle), gazing as with one eye upon the face of Hakuo.

Hakuo said : " I have let you speak the vile language which filled your heart (belly). Have you nothing more than this to say " ?

Babiman said : " No ! There are mountains that I might say, but my thoughts are in the main like this."

Hakuo said : " That the person you call Jesus was an ancient God from eternal ages,— that he appeared before the production of all things,—that he made man,—that he made prayer by which all who repeat it, after death, may ascend to heaven—you may say it, but that they ascend to heaven I do not believe." Babiman only hung his head, while Hakuo, laughing, satirically continued : " Jesus appears to me to have been very foolish ; far better would it have been for him not to make man at all, than, for man's sake, to endure such bitter suffering, and with so many hard and painful works to make a prayer, by repeating which, men might get to heaven. A god that makes me without my asking it, if he suffers my pains, only gets what he deserves ; more than this, to make man who is capable of committing so much wickedness, is to be a god who commits the sin of murder, but we will pass on to other points. In all the classics of the three kingdoms (of China, Japan and India), in the sacred books of Shaka, or in the historical books, not a word is said about Jesus creating all living things ; they have never heard even of his name ; truly then this is a heritical doctrine. When Buddha was on earth there were false teachers who opposed the true religion, despised God, and disputed often with the disciples of Buddha, but never could get any advantage over the true religion. That you were not smitten with punishment when you abused the sacred books of Shaka is just for the same reason that cats and rats are not punishable when they eat the image of Buddha and his sacred books; which is, that they are naturally beasts and why should you, a false teacher, the same as a beast, be smitten with punishment? If you have any proofs able to defeat the true religion, if only one word, or one sentence, spit them out, and I will answer them," said he, striking the mat and leaning towards him. Babiman had not a word to say in reply, but he became red in the face.

Hakuo said again: "You are like one who deceives the foolish people of the world. Let me see you, by your miraculous skill, show what the appearance is of one who in this life becomes divine." But Babiman was like a dumb person and hung his head. After a little, he arose, saying, "Alas what a bad man you are, it is hard to have anything to do with such an one as you; those who will not believe cannot be saved." He then went out grumbling, like a dog running away howling. Hakuo cried out: "You vile heretic! I am surprised still more that you should utter those golden words of Shaka, 'Those who will not believe cannot be saved.' Wait a little and answer me." So saying, he laid hold of the skirt of his robe to detain him; but it rent and he, escaping, left.

The whole assembly rejoiced, but especially the old mother, saying, "How superior is the true religion to all others."

Hakuo said: "As that religion has been so much promulgated, I verily thought that the discussion to-day would be a difficult one, even to the quoting from the sacred book of Shaka and the laws of Astronomy and Geography; but contrary to all my expectations, he has done nothing but use foul and abusive language, praising himself and despising others, so that I had to reply to him in the same way. I am more and more convinced that it is a bad religion. I hope the time will soon come when the Shogun will prohibit it." After conversing upon various subjects connected with Buddhism, Hakuo took his leave and returned to Miako.

A few days after this, Shuri, getting a short leave of absence from the Castle Yodo, returned to his mother's house. Every person he met told him about the late discussion between Babiman and Hakuo. He thought it a strange affair, so after he returned to the castle, for the entertainment of Hideyoshi, he told it to him. When Hideyoshi heard it he said: "That is right. I have all along known that that religion was bad; when that religion first came, in the time of Nobunaga, I was present at the meeting when the Padres requested permission to promulgate it, and heard the whole matter; and also afterwards, when he called a council of his ministers and learned men, and they all advised that they should not be allowed to propagate it; but Nobunaga would not listen to them. At last he built Namban monastery, and the sect spread more and more, until the nobles and the military class were all carried away with it. Nobunaga even regretted it afterwards and spoke privately of suppressing it, but having to take his army to put down the rebellion of Murashige[118] he had to let the matter rest. Having been unmolested from that time until now, its followers have become still more numerous. But I am convinced it is a bad religion and that it should not be suffered to go on; Namban monastery must be destroyed, and the religion exterminated." So said Hideyoshi, and all his ministers agreed with him, advising him to crucify the two Padres, the Romans, and those living with them, and that all others should suffer decapitation. Hideyoshi replied that indeed what they advised was quite proper, but that it would be better to send the foreigners back to their own country. The whole assembly of nobles with one voice said:

" In the reign of Gota the 90th Emperor.[119] the Mongols,

---

118 See note 89, page 30.

119 Go-uda (後宇多) A.D. 1275–1287.

with an army of several myriads, and 500 ships, landed on the coast of Kiushu and attacked that country. But the great nobles of the western provinces defeated them, and took their Commander-in cheif Ajiyo[120] a prisoner, and sent him to Kamakura. The Emperor, Yaszshin[121] committed every thing to Tokimune,[122] and by Tokimune's advice Ajiyo's head was cut off on the sea back of Yui ; this would be a good precedent for your Majesty to to follow in this case."

Hideyoshi replied : " True, but after that, the Mongols came again in the 4th year of Koan,[123] with an army of many myriads and four hundred ships, and attacked Kiushu. The great nobles of the western provinces tried to drive them off but were unable, for these Mongols fought with desperation. Couriers were dispatched to Kiyoto and Kamakura, one after another, like one running his finger over the teeth of a comb. The Emperor was alarmed and sent a messenger to the temple of Ize[124] to offer prayers to the God of the Wind, saying 'The wares that come from foreign countries are the wares of wicked demons, blow them back, O God of Winds' when most marvellously, from the altar of the God there arose a wind like a little smoke, which in the western provinces blow away large trees and huge stones, and raised such a storm in the ocean that the 400 ships of the Mongols were wrecked in every direction, and more than half of the army sank to the bottom

---

120 Ajiro (アジロウ) in the Japanese text.

121 According to history "Koreyasu Shinno" or Prince Koreyasu was Shogun at Kamakura under the Hojo Regents from 1266–1289 A.D.

122 Tokimune of the Hojo Family (北條氏), which ruled Japan from 1256 to 1284. During this period there was the curious spectacle of a *defacto* ruler, a Hojo Regent, acting in the name of a puppet Shogun, who drew his legal authority from the Emperor in name at Kyoto.

123 Koan (弘安); A.D. 1278–1287.

124 Ise, (伊勢), where the ancestral shrines of the Imperial Family are situated ; the reference is to the storm which destroyed the invading fleet of the Mongols in 1281, an occurrence very similar to the attempted invasion of England by the Spanish Armada, which was also scattered by a tempest.

of the sea; the rest fled back to their own country. Those were put into ships that were left and sent back home. This also may serve as a precedent. It will be much better to incline to mercy and pity and send the Padres back to their own country."

Now, besides Ishida, Konishi and Takayama,[125] amongst the officers of Hideyoshi, twenty-three had become followers of this sect. So they secretly sent word to Namban monastery. This caused the greatest commotion, turning everything upside down. The three men Babiman, Goszna and Gunmon fled where they best could. Maszda and Nagatszka,[126] having received orders from Hideyoshi, went to the Namban monastery and arrested the four men Urugan, Furaten, Gerido and Yaisz, and having destroyed the monastery, returned.

These four Padres were afterwards put on board a Holland ship and sent back to their own country. Their followers after they were examined were commanded to recant. All those who would not recant were executed, so that the Christian sect was completely destroyed.

Babiman fled to Amakusa in the province of Hizen where he published religion. Goszmo[127] fled to the province of Yenshu.[128] After four years had elapsed he changed his name to Shoszhe and lived in the town of Nakahama in the province of Senshu, where he practiced surgery. Gunmon fled and concealed

---

125 Ishida Mitsunari (石田三成)—a famous general under Hideyoshi by whom he was much trusted. On the death of his Master he supported his son Hideyori, but was defeated with his supporters by Iyeyasu Tokugawa, the first Shogun or Military Chief of that family, at the battle of Sekigahara.

Konishi Yukinaga (小西行長) one of the so-called Christian Daimyo; he took a prominent part in the war of Hideyoshi against Korea and had a Fief in Kyushiu.

Takayama, see page 30 and note 91.

126 Mayeda, see page 29 and note 88.

Nagatsuka (長束), possibly an error for Nagahide, see page 16 note 36.

127 Cosmo, see page 27 and note 84.

128 Ichihashi Shosuke (一橋庄助) in the Japanese text.

himself in the province of Yechizen.[129] He also, after the lapse of four years, changed his name to Seizn[130] and became a physician and lived in Nakahama.

Now, in 16th year of Tensho and 9th month, the citizens of Shenshu by the name of Toran and Goyu,[131] came to the castle of Fushimi, to pay their respects to Hideyoshi. These men were fashionable tea-makers, and would usually tell to Hideyoshi the current gossip of the country. When Hideyoshi enquired of them what news there was, they replied that in Nakahama there were the men, one a surgeon called Shoszke, the other a physician called Seian, who besides treating diseases, did many strange things. They were especially famous for their sleight of hand, and had a great reputation for the doing of many miraculous things.

When Hideyoshi heard it, he ordered Hentemon[132] to send for them quickly, that he might see their skill. After three days he returned bringing them with him, and being called into the presence of Hideyoshi, he said to them: "Let me see you do some of your wonderful things for my amusement."

They humbly bowed in consent. The first was, to fill a large bowl with water, then cutting paper into diamond shapes he threw them into the water when they immediately became fishes and swan about like real fish; after a little while they became like the original paper. Not to speak of his ministers, his whole family, who were looking on, regarded it as a miracle. Next, telling the ladies that they must not be alarmed, he took from his bosom a paper string, cut off a piece three feet long, and threw it on the floor, repeating an incantation; immediately it became a snake and moved about. The ladies made

---

129 Echizen (越前).

130 Shimada Seian (嶋田清庵) in the Japanese text.

131 Senshu, *i.e.* Izumi-no-kuni; in the Japanese text the names of the two men are given as Tennojiya Shuchin (天王寺屋宗珍) and Aburaya Joyu (油屋常祐) of Sakai.

132 Sasaki Heiyemon (佐々木平右衛門).

a great outcry, and as it was not a proper thing to be in a parlour, he again repeated his incantation, and it was restored to the original paper string. He next put some sand in a wine cup and taking some millet seeds sprinked them upon the sand, when they became ants, moving about and creeping out. Again, taking an egg, he held it in his hand, repeating his incantation; when he opened his hand, it was a young chick and crowed; repeating his incatation, it became an egg again.

The ladies never having seen Fujiyama, requested that it might be shown to them. As it was large, it was impossible to show it in the parlour, so they said they would do it in the garden. The men then went out of the library reciting an incantation. "Look then", said they, opening the screens, and sure enough there was the real unmistakable Fujiyama plainly in the distance. Next, they said they would show them the eight finest prospects in the province of Omi. Shutting the screens, they said over their incantations; when the screens were opened, the whole eight prospects were pictured before their eyes. All regarded these things with wonder. Then, Hideyoshi requesting it, they showed him the view of Aka-ishi in the province of Shenshu. Hideyoshi said again: "I have only heard tell of a ghost, but have never seen one; if there is such a thing, let me see it." The men, bowing humbly, consented and said: "A ghost is a thing that does not appear in the day time, but at night when it becomes dark we will do this for you." Hideyoshi replied that their request was reasonable, and commanded that they should rest, and had various refreshments provided for them. They all considered it a rare sight, and waited impatiently for the evening. The sun having set, and the night well set in, all the candles were put out except one dim light in the parlour. It was the 18th night of the 9th month; the moon shone only about the garden, the parlour was dark and it was a time when one is apt to feel timid. The two men went outside the door and repeated the usual incantation; after a little delay, they came inside, and joining hands, sat in quiet abstraction. The moon that had until now been shining, suddenly became clouded and the yard dark, so that nothing could be distinctly seen, when what seemed like a puff of wind passed up, and from the shade of some bushes issued forth a ghost, appearing like a woman dressed in white, with dishevelled hair and holding a staff. It gradually approached the library. Hideyoshi quickly looked at it by the aid of a light, when he knew her to be a concubine, called Kiku, who belonged to him when he was yet called Tokiehito.[133] When he became Shogun she came seeking for him, and prayed again to be taken into his service, but as she had formerly vilified him and said many things against him, he would not receive her; wherefore she said many things to excite his resentment, and as a last resource he had her executed.

Now when these men, knowing these things, caused her to appear, he felt they must be suspicious fellows. Feeling very much out of humour he ordered the exhibition to be at once stopped; so the men, making passes with their hands and repeating the incantation, the ghost disappeared.

They were then called into the parlour. The men were glad, supposing that it was for the purpose of bestowing rewards upon them, and came in; when, contrary to their expectations, he ordered two constables to lay hold of them and bind them with a rope. They were at once bound, and Hideyoshi said to them:

" This day's performances are certainly most extraordinary, but knowing how disagreeable it must be to me for you to bring up such a ghost, convinces me that you are suspicious fellows. A few years ago when the Christain sect was destroyed, Babiman, Goszmo and Gunmon[134] escaped and it was not known where they had gone, but I am sure you must be the men."

---

133 Kinoshita Tokichi (木下藤吉). The name of Hideyoshi when he was young and unknown.

134 See notes 79, 84, and 85 on page 27.

He had them strictly examined, and it was found that his suspicions were true, and they confessed themselves to be Goszmo and Gunmon. If such persons as these were suffered to live what might they not do? So he had both of them executed at Awata.[135]

After this, when official examination was made in every place, as there were a great many who honoured this religion, they would apparently adjure it but secretly hang up the picture of Jesus. Hideyoshi ordered that every one should be seized and bound, and that those who truly recanted should be spared, but those who would not should be executed. Thus by the severity of the goverment the sect was exterminated.

Twenty-four years after this, the 16th year of Keicho, Kiyo-masa,[136] Prince of Higo, died. The disciples of Babiman, regarding this as fortunate, propagated this religion in the country of Uto,[137] in the province of Higo, and the followers became numerous. In this province, in the village of Fusui, there was a Buddhist temple called Jitszkoji.[138] This temple they tore down, and drove the priest, named Shinzosz,[139] away. Shinzosz, enraged, went to Yedo, and complaining to the superintendent of Temples, under Hidetada the Shogun,[140] this country was soon quieted.

After this, in the 3rd year of the era called K'wanyei,[141]

---

135 Awata-guchi (粟田口).

136 Kato Higo-no-kami Kiyomasa (加藤肥後守清正).
Kato Kiycmasa was a staunch adherent of Buddhism and is always much reviled in the Letters from the missionaries. Like the Christian Daimyos who would allow none but Christians in their territories, he in his would have none but Buddhists.
Keicho (慶長) era A.D. 1596–1614.

137 Uto-gun (宇土郡) in Kumamoto-ken.

138 Jikkoji (實向寺)

139 Shinzosu (眞藏主).

140 Hidetada, the second Shogun of the Tokugawa Family; it was he who finally decided on the suppressson of Christianity and the banishment of the missionaries.

141 Kanyei (寛永) A.D. 1624–1643.

there was a begging priest who travelled about the provinces of Omi and Tamba, who, by showing a mirror, or giving alms, recommended this religion; on this account there were again many followers. At that time Itakura-Iga-nokami-Hatszshige[142] was appointed at Kiyoto to judge in this matter, but there being so many foolish people who were determined to throw away their lives, he could not finish it, wherefore Okubosagami-no-kami was appointed to be the judge of the Christians, by the Shogun. He went to Kiyoto and seized every one of the followers of this sect, put them into bags, binding them strongly and allowing their heads only to project. They were then taken down to the river bank, and although they were told by the officers that all who recanted should be spared, at first they would not listen. " O, how great is the love of Jesus; if our bodies should be cut to pieces, we shall immediately ascend to heaven," they said, repeating a prayer; but the greater part of them would not recant. The officers promised that if any amongst them desired to recant and would get a certificate from any Buddhist Temple, they should yet be saved; but notwithstanding all these offers, every one refused to turn, so they were bound in bags, piled up one on top of another, and burnt.

Again, in Szmotake,[143] in the province of Omi, this sect arose. This was owing to some disciples of Babiman who resided a short time in this province; but as the government was very vigilant it was soon suppressed. After this there were no more of this sect.

Now, at Osaka there were three persons who would not recant; two of them of the same family—Shishibeyo[144] and

---

142 Itakura Iga-no-Kami Katsushige (板倉伊賀守勝重) was Governor of Kyoto from 1601 to 1621.

Okubo Sagami-no-Kami (大久保相模守) was suspected of favouring Christianity and was sent to Kyoto to persecute Christians in order to prove him.

143 Sumitake (すみ竹).

144 Shichibyoye (七兵衛); Hachiyemon (八右衛門).

Hachiyamon—were crucified with their heads downwards. The other, Sokichi,[145] was killed with the water torture.[146]

At Kiyoto there were four men who would not recant; two of them were crucified and two were drawn with oxen.

Thirteen years after this, in the reign of Iyemitsz,[147] the Shogun, in the 14th year of the era K'wanyei, there was a revolt in Amakusa in the province of Hizen. At this time also the Christians were many, and more than 37,000 persons were slain. This is more minutely detailed in the history of Shimabara and will be omitted here. After this, a most stringent edict was enacted, prohibiting this religion, ordering that every year, spring and fall, there should be an examination for this sect, especially at Nagasaki, where the Governor in the first month of each year, at the time of making inquisition, caused every one without exception to tread on a picture of Jesus.[148]

---

145 Sokichi (惣吉).

146 Water torture, *i.e.* water was poured down the throat until death took place.

147 Iyemitsu (家光). The third Shogun of the Tokugawa Family who ruled from 1623 to 1651. It was under him that the final step of closing the country was taken.

148 Fumie (踏繪) *lit* treading picture. In order to detect Christians every year the people of Nagasaki and district had to appear before the census officers and tread on a brass figure of "Our Lord"; if they refused it was taken to mean that they were adherents of Christianity.

PART II.

The following account of the Shimabara Rebellion, with a mention of which the " Real Record of Christianity " ends, is taken from a copy of the *Far East*, a magazine once published in Yokohama. Neither the original text nor the name of the translator is known, but many passages agree in parts with the several texts of the undermentioned Japanese works, so that, although none can be accepted as the true original, all are sufficiently alike to allow the identification of names and places.

1. Shimabara Kassen-ki (島原合戰記)

2. Amakusa Monogatari (天草物語)

The above Shimabara Kassen-ki (the Record of Battles at Shimabara) and Amakusa Monogatari (The Tales of Amakusa) differ in titles and illustrations, but the text of both is the same. Examining the two copies carefully, it appears that the original title of both was " Shimabara-ki " (島原記: the Record of Shimabara), and they were made from its original woodcut, with different names on the title pages. According to the preface of both pamphlets, though anonymous, the author was a native of Osaka (Naniwa). When the riot arose he happened to be in Kyushu, and during the riot he made a trip to the places concerned. The riot continued from Oct. 1637 (A.D.) to Feb. 1638 (A.D.) and the book " Shimabara-ki " was written in 1640 (A.D.) at Yedo (granting that the word "江城" means "江戶城" (Yedojo). It is stated in the preface that the author's purpose was to give information about the riot to his friends in Osaka.

Both the Kanbun Shoseki Mokuroku (Catalogue of books of the Kanbun Era), published in 1670, and the Genroku Shoseki Mokuroku (Catalogue of books of the Genroku Era), published in 1692, mention the Shimabara-ki (in the former) and the Shimabara Kassen-ki (in the latter), and it is conceivable that the Shimabara-ki was published very soon after the riot was suppressed. Both 1 and 2 of the above contain sixteen chapters each.

3. Amakusa Sodo (天草騒動).

The Amakusa Sodo (the Amakusa Disturbances) is a reprint made by the Waseda University in 1918, which contains 68 chapters. Its author is unknown. The first part of this book treats of matters relative to the Nanbanji in Kyoto, but most of the chapters are detailed accounts of the Amakusa riot.

4. Nanto Henran-ki (南島變亂記).

The Nanto Henran-ki (the Record of Riot of the Southern Island) is a reprint made in 1914 in Tokyo. The original copy seems to consist of 30 volumes. The author is unknown, but, according to the last part of the book, it was written in Kyoto in 1782, based on various records about the Shimabara riot.

5. Shimabara-Amakusa Nikki (島原天草日記).

The author of this book "Shimabara-Amakusa Nikki" (the Diary of Shimabara and Amakusa) is Matsudaira Kai-no-kami Terutsuna, the heir of Matsudaira Izu-no-kami Nobutsuna. Terutsuna was taken to Shimabara at the time of the riot by his father Nobutsuna; he was a young man of 19 years of age. According to the preface of the book, Terutsuna noted down a very minute account of his trip to Kyushu, but this valuable record was destroyed by the great fire which took place at Yedo in 1657 (when over 108,000 men and women were killed) and in 1663 (Kanbun 3rd year), when Terutsuna was 45 years old, he rewrote his diary from memory. The existing diary is the one rewritten by Terutsuna in 1663.

6. Shimabara Ikki Matsukura-ki (島原一揆松倉記).

This Shimabara Ikki Matsukura-ki (The Matsukura's Record of the Shimabara Riot) is supposed to have been recorded by Matsukura Nagato-no-kami or his retainer during the period of the riot.

The Shimabara Rebellion is so called from the peninsula of the name where the outbreak first occurred. Like the neck of land on which Nagasaki stands, it is hilly and inaccessible except from the sea. Both Shimabara and the nearby island of Amakusa were early centres of Christianity and when the persecution began it was to these wild spots that the unbroken followers of Christ fled. Beyond defiefing the Christian Lords of these districts, the Government at Yedo showed at first little inclination to hunt them down. Foreign accounts have it that the rebellion was due to the heavy taxation levied by the new Lords of the two Fiefs, but Japanese tradition has it that the outbreak was purely Christian in character based on the expected appearance of a Saviour whose arrival had been prophecied.

The truth is that in these districts were gathered all that was best of Japan's Christians. Hither had fled the samurai who preferred to lose all rather than recant. It may be that the cruel exactions of tax collectors ignited the spark, but what laid the fire ready for kindling was ambition. The twenty thousand men that defended Hara Castle for six months against the hosts of all Kyushu were not just farmers and peasants driven to despair; they were men or the sons of men who had fought under the banners of Christian Lords like Konishi Yukinaga, Takayama Ukon, Kuroda Yoshitaka and other Christian leaders, veterans of the Korean and Japanese civil wars. To submit without striking a blow would have been foreign to their natures. Flimsy though their chances, they preferred to stake their all. Victory meant power, defeat death, which was infinitely preferable to the life they were leading.

As history relates, the rebellion was crushed but not without a fierce struggle. To-day monuments[1] mark the sites where brave men fell. Firstly, on the battle ground at Hara Castle there is the " Tomb of Bones " which tradition says contains the bones of the killed on both sides. Nearby is a stone erected in memory of Itakura Shigemasa, the Commander of the Government forces, who lost his life in the first attack. At Tomioka, in the Island of Amakusa, stands another stone marking, it is said, the place where those taken alive were executed and buried. In Nagasaki itself, at the approach to Tateyama Hill, stands a small monument fronting a tiny plot of land in which are buried the heads of the vanquished brought from the battlefield as a warning to all who would believe in Christ. It is remarkable that no man has been found hardy enough to build on the spot, which remains vacant hidden among the houses. So strong is local tradition.

1 See illustrations at the end of the book.

THE SHIMABARA REBELLION.

CHAPTER I.

ACCOUNT OF THE INSURRECTION OF CHRISTIANS AT SHIMABARA[149].

The Christians first landed, from a Chinese ship, on the Western coast, and propagated their doctrines in the cycle of Tenbun[150] (1532-1554) during the reign of the Mikado Go-narano-in[151] (104th Emperor). After that, in the 19th year of Eroku[152] (1666)—Eiroku, 1558-1569—in the time of Mikado Ogimachino-in[153] (105th Emperor), a foreign ship was driven ashore on the Cape of Mioora[154] in Sagami[155]. There were many Christians on board, and these propagated their doctrines.

---

149 Shimabara (島原) is within Minami-Takagi-gun (南高來郡), Hizen (肥前), Nagasaki-ken (長崎縣).

150 Tenbun (天文) is the name of an era of the Mikado Go-Nara covering the period from A.D. 1532 to 1554.

151 Gonarano-in refers to the 104th Mikado Go-Nara (後奈良天皇), whose reign was from A.D. 1527 to 1557.

152 Eroku is for Eiroku (永祿), 1558-1569, which is the name of an era of the 105th Mikado Ogimachi (正親町天皇), 1558-1586. The phrase in the text "in the 19th year of Eiroku (1666)" seems to be a mistake, because there is no "19th year" in the era of Eiroku. The year "1666" corresponds to the 6th year of Kanbun (寛文), belonging to the reign of the 111th Mikado Reigen (靈元天皇).

153 Ogimachino-in is for the 105th Mikado Ogimachi (正親町天皇), whose reign was from A.D. 1558 to 1586.

154 Cape of Mioora seems to mean the Miura Peninsula (Miura-Hanto 三浦半島).

155 Sagami is now in Kanagawa-ken. (Sagami=相模).

Thereupon the Shogun, Hojo Sakyo-no-daibu Oojiyasu[156], called them to Odawara[157] and let them reside there. At this time, all the Western countries of Japan had received the Christian doctrines. Thus the true doctrine was corrupted by the false; money was given to lead men to unite with the Sect; Buddhism was opposed; the foolish were imposed upon by strange arts. Anarchy was imminent by reason of secret societies of men who aimed to subvert the government. Therefore in the Cycle of Bunroku (1592-1596) the Prime Minister Hideyoshi[158], being greatly incensed at this, sought out the disciples, and having taken and bound more than twenty of the head men, he sent them along the main road, to the port of Nagasaki, in Hizen,[159] where they were crucified. Still, those who remained continued to live in the Western countries, where they ceased not to mislead the people.

In consequence of this, the Shogun Iyeyasu,[160] in order to suppress them, on the 21st day of the 6th month of the 19th year of Keicho (1614)[161] commanded Tatara Yoshihiro

---

156 Hojo Sakyo-no-daibu Oojiyasu stands for Hojo Sakyo-no-taibu Ujiyasu. (北條左京大夫氏康) "Hojo" is Ujiyasu's family name, "Sakyo-no-taibu" his official title, and "Ujiyasu" his personal name.

157 Odawara (小田原) is in Sagami of Kanagawa-ken.

158 Hideyoshi: Toyotomi Hideyoshi (豐臣秀吉), otherwise Taiko (太閤) or Taiko-san (太閤樣).

159 Hizen (肥前) belongs partly to Nagasaki-ken and partly to Saga-ken. This execution is known to Church History as the martyrdom of the Twenty-Six Saints 1597.

160 Shogun Iyeyasu. The Shogun Tokugawa Iyeyasu (將軍德川家康), the 1st Shogun of the Tokugawa Shogunate. The term "shogun" is an abbreviation of "Sei-I-Taishogun" (征夷大將軍), which means "the Generalissimo for the Subjugation of Barbarians". Iyeyasu acquired this office in A.D. 1603.

161 Keicho (慶長) is the name of an era 1596-1614 partly in the reign of the 105th Mikado Go-Yozei (後陽成天皇), who reigned from A.D. 1587 to 1611 and partly in the reign of the Mikado Go-Mizuno-o 1611-1629.

Yamaguchi Suruga-no-kami[162] to examine and punish the sect, and the heads of some were cut off and exposed at the corners of streets, while others were driven to foreign lands. Hence those doctrines for a long time languished. But again, in the latter part of the 10th month of the 14th year of Kanei[163] (1637), the villagers of Shimabara, in the district of Takaji,[164] in Hizen, embraced the Christian doctrines, and concocted a conspiracy, which terminated in rebellion. When we inquire as to its origin we find that Oye Matsemon,[165] Chidzuka-Zenzaimon[166]

162 Tatara Yoshihiro Yamaguchi Suruga-no-Kami 多多良義弘 山口駿河守. Although this appears to be a combination of two different persons, it is really one person's name. The record "Nagasaki Engi Ryakki" (長崎縁起略記: the Epitome of Historical Affairs of Nagasaki) states that Yamaguchi Suruga-no-Kami Shigehiro (山口駿河守重弘) left Fushimi (伏見) on June 21st in the 19th year of Keicho (1614) and arrived at Nagasaki on July 22nd; this Yamaguchi Suruga-no-Kami Shigehiro must be identical with Tatara Yoshihiro Yamaguchi Suruga-no-Kami. Tatara is his first family name, (Tatara=多多良) Shigehiro (or Yoshihiro) his personal name, and Suruga-no-Kami means that he had the title of Governor of Suruga (駿河守); Yamaguchi is his second family name. (Yamaguchi=山口).

Some historical documents consulted, however, show that there was no person named either Shigehiro (重弘) or Yoshihiro (義弘) in the lineage of the Yamaguchi family, but there was a person named Shigemasa (重政), who seems to be identical with Yamaguchi Suruga-no-Kami Shigehiro. "Masa 政" and "Hiro 弘" are very confusing when they are written in the cursive style.

163 Kanei is for Kan-ei (寛永), 1624-1643, which is the name of the era of part of the reign of the 107th Mikado Go-Mizuno-o (後水尾天皇), 1612-1629 and partly of the Mikado (Empress) Meisho 1629-1643.

164 Takaji, the present Takagi-gun in Nagasaki-ken. This "gun" (郡) is now politically divided into two parts, namely, "Minami-Takagi-gun" (南高来郡) and the "Kita-Takagi-gun" (北高来郡); the former means the southern part of Takagi, while the latter the northern part of it. According to some old books, Takagi (高来) was sometimes called "Takaku" and the characters "高久" were given for it; Shimabara is now called "Shimabara-machi" (島原町), which is in the southern part of Takagi.

165 Oye Matsemon is for Oye Matsu-e-mon (大江松右衛門). This person must be identical with Oye Matsu-e-mon, or sometimes Oye Moku-e-mon (大江杢右衛門). When the character "Matsu 松", it written in the fashion "枩" instead of "松", it resembles "Moku 杢". For this reason "Matsu" and "Moku" are confusing when they are written in the cursive style. It is unknown which was his real name, Matsu-e-mon or Moku-e-mon.

166 Chidzuka Zenzaimon: Chizuka Zenza-e-mon (千束善左衛門).

Oye-Genemon,[167] Mori-Soiken[168] Yama-Zenzaimon,[169] and others, villagers of that place, were all leaders of the conspirators. These had formerly been retainers of Konishi Sets-nokami Yukinaga.[170] This Yukinaga had taken part in the rebellion of Ishida Jibushoyou Mitsunari,[171] and on the 15th of the 9th month of the 5th year of Keicho (1600) was defeated at the battle of Awono,[172] in Noshu, and, being captured, was executed and his retainers were scattered and concealed in various places. The above five men lived in Oyano and Chidzuka, in the district of Amakusa in Higo, but for a short time also lived concealed in Fukaie-mura[174] in Shimabara in Hizen. They having held a consultation, collected the neighbouring villagers, and privately addressed them as follows:—" Some years ago when the sect of Jesus was prohibited, there was a priest in Kamitsura in Amakusa, who, when he was driven to foreign

---

167 Oye Genemon: Oye Gen-u-e-mon (大江源右衛門).

168 Mori Soiken (森宗意軒) seems to be identical with Mori Soi Anryuken appearing in the record "Nanto-Henran-Ki" (the Record of Riot in the Southern Island: 南島變亂記), who was a son of Mori Choi (森長意), a physician in Osaka. The said record states that it is wrong to call him "Mori Soiken" as Mori (森) is his family name, his personal name being Soi (宗意) and his pen name Anryuken (安龍軒).

169 Yama Zenzaimon is for Yama Zenza-e-mon (山善左衛門).

170 Konishi Sets-nokami Yukinaga is for Konishi Settsu-no-Kami Yukinaga (小西攝津守行長). He was one of the best known generals of Toyotomi Hideyoshi. Settsu-no-Kami or Lord of Settsu was his title. He was a Christian Daimyo, his fief being Higo province in Kyushu; he sided against Iyeyasu Tokugawa, was one of the vanquished at Sekigahara, and was executed at Kyoto in 1600. The missionaries call him Don Augustin, under which name he was baptised in 1583.

171 Ishida Jibushoyou Mitsunari is for Ishida Jibushoyu Mitsunari (石田治部少輔三成). Jibushoyu is an official title. He was executed by Iyeyasu Tokugawa after the battle of Sekigahara.

172 The Battle of Awono means the battle at Aonogahara (青野原), which took place after Sekigahara.

173 Noshu (濃州) is for Mino (美濃), now Gifu-ken.

174 Fukaiemura is for Fuka-e-mura (深江村).

lands, left a book of one volume called Hankan[175] (Mirror of the Future). When we open this book we read as follows: 'Hereafter when five in five* years have passed, a remarkable youth will appear in Japan. He, without study, will acquire all knowledge. This will certainly come to pass. Then the clouds will be bright along the East and West. A wisteria flower will bloom from a dead tree. All men will wear the sign of the cross upon their heads, and white flags will flutter on the sea, on rivers, mountains and plains. Then the time of honouring Jesus will arrive, &c.,' We now learn, they said, from this book that the time referred to is this present year. Many clouds are now bright in the East and West. Also a

---

175 Hankan: This word appears in historical documents relative to the Shimabara Riot in three different forms:

1. Hankan (半鑑).
2. Mikan (未鑑) in the said record (the Record of Riot in the Southern Island).
3. Batsukan (末鑑) in the record "Amakusa Monogatari" (Tales of Amakusa 天草物語).

According to the second one, the Mikan seems to be an abbreviation of Mirai-kan (未來鑑), which means the "Mirror" through which one can see affairs occurring in the "future". But, according to the third one, the Batsukan (or Matsukan) seems to mean "Suye-no-Kagami" (末の鑑). The "Mi 未" (Imada or Mada in Japanese) and "Batsu 末 or Matsu" (Suye in Japanese) are two different Chinese Characters, but they sometimes mean the same thing (the future). The "Mi" means "future" when it is combined with "Rai" (來), making one phrase or word "Mirai" (未來 the future). The character "Matsu or Batsu" (末) and its Japanese reading "Suye" (末) also mean the "future" as seen in the following:

Suye-no-yo (末の世)=future world.
Masse (末 世)=future world.
(Matsu-se)
Yo-no-suye (世の末)=future of the humanity.
Matsudai (末 代)=future generations.

For the above reasons, it is conjectured that the English translator of the "Shimabara" might have taken the Chinese characters "Mi" (未), or "Matsu 末 (or Batsu)", written in their cursive styles, for the character "Han" (半), which has no sense of "future", and translated the word "Hankan" (半鑑) by the context of the words into "Mirror of the future", because these three Chinese characters are very much alike when they are written in the cursive style.

* This may mean 55, or 5 by 5=25.

red wisteria has blossomed on a cherry tree in the garden of Oye Genemon (one of the five conspirators). He who, without study, understands all sciences is a youth called Shiro,[176] eldest son of Jimbei of Amakusa—one who, though young, is without an equal in understanding and learning. The time has then already come. Let every one, disregarding the prohibition of the Government, espouse the cause of Jesus. If we incur the displeasure of The Shogun, is it not still our chief desire, having sacrificed our lives for our religion, to obtain the reward of Heaven after death?"

When they, with much wisdom and eloquence, had spoken thus, the villagers there present, many of whom were secretly

---

176 Shiro (四郎). This person is known differently in various historical documents relative to the Shimabara and Amakusa Riots. The following are his best known names:

1. Amakusa Shiro (天草四郎).
2. Shiro Tayu Tokisada (四郎太夫時貞).
3. Shiro Tokisada (四郎時貞).
4. Amakusa Shiro Tokisada (天草四郎時貞).
5. Ju-shii Hizen-no-Kami Shirotayu Watanabe Tokisada (従四位肥前守四郎太夫渡邊時貞).
6. Oyano Shiro (大矢野四郎).

Shiro=His first personal name (in his childhood).

Amakusa=Amakusa-gun in Kumamoto-ken; Shiro was born at Oyano village in Amakusa-gun, and for this reason, the term Amakusa is used as if it was his family name; such was very common in Japan in olden days.

Tayu=self-assumed title taken by Shiro himself.

Tokisada=his second personal name.

Ju-shii Hizen-no-Kami=the Governor of Hizen (with the secondary 4th Court Rank); this was the office of the Prince of Satsuma in those days, and Shiro assumed this office (or rank) falsely.

Oyano=the village where Shiro was born.

In this English text of "Shimabara" Amakusa Jimbei is said to be Shiro's father, but, in the "Record of Riot in the Southern Island," Watanabe Kozaemon (渡邊小左衛門) is mentioned as his father, and Shiro's mother, namely, Watanabe Kozaemon's wife, is given as a younger sister of Amakusa Jimbei. Should this be correct we are able to see why Shiro was called "Watanabe Tokisada" as above in the 5th of his names. In the "Nagasaki Engi Ryakki," (長崎緣起略記) it is mentioned that the real family name of Amakusa Jimbei was Matsuda, and Shiro is mentioned in the same book as Masuda Shiro (益田四郎).

attached to this religion, united themselves with the speakers. There was also a man called Sashi Kizaimon[177] in Fukaiemura, who had been a member of this sect for several years. He had in his possession an old picture of "Deus,"[178] but fearing the government prohibition, he hid it away in a chest, and as the picture had no border, he for a long time had been anxious to obtain a border for it. In the meantime, the picture, in one night, was mysteriously provided with a border, such as he had desired. The man Sashi greatly rejoiced, and related this fact to the people of the adjoining villages. This rumour spread, and the people assembled at the house of Sashi, where, the picture being hung up, they worshipped it and were filled with wonder, and united in exalting that sect more and more.

At that time a retainer of the lord of the castle of Takaji Matsukura Nagato-no-kami Katsuiye[179] named Haiashi Hyoemon,[180] Governor of the villages, hearing of this matter, hastened to Fukaiemura on the 25th of the 10th month, and when he had entered the house of Sashi and looked around he found a number of the villagers seated in order conversing about Jesus. Haiashi became very angry, reproved them for the crime of violating the laws of the government, beat some of the fellows in the company, tore down their divinity (the picture), put it into the fire and reduced it to ashes. The whole assembly was greatly enraged and beat Haiashi 林 to

---

177 This seems to be identical with "Sashiki Sajiemon" (佐志木佐治右衛門).

178 The Jesuits, for want of a good translation in Japanese for "God", retained the Latin "Deus."

179 The Matsukura family was given the Fief of Shimabara in 1615, when the former Christian Daimyo, Arima Naozumi, apostatized and was moved to Nobeoka in Hyuga. His Christian name was Michael and he was the son of Arima Harunobu, the John Protasius of the Jesuits. Harunobu is known for the attack and capture of the Portuguese galleon "Madre de Dios" in Nagasaki Harbour, 1609, of which some guns have lately been salved.

180 Haiashi is for Hayashi (林).

death on the spot. His followers with difficulty escaped death, and returned to the Castle of Takaji. The villagers consulted together, and they knew that when this matter should be reported to the lord of the land he would without doubt assail them; and they knew also that preparation must be made so as not easily to fall into the hands of the assailants; so they returned to their homes, polished their spear points, prepared powder and ball, and waited to be attacked.

CHAPTER II.

Troops sent to Fukae-mura; Villagers approach the Castle of Takaji.

On the night of the 25th of the 10th month, the followers of the Governor Haiashi Hyoemon escaped to the Castle of Takaji and minutely related the affair of Fukaie-mura. At the time the lord of the castle, Matsukura Nagato-no-kami Katsuiye,[181] and his brother Ookon Katsushige resided together in Yedo; hence, by the order of Tanaka Sodayou and Okamoto Shimbei who had charge of the castle, fifteen mounted soldiers, eightly men armed with muskets, and about three hundred foot soldiers, were chosen to attack the villagers. These left the castle in the night, and about day-light on the morning of the 26th of the 10th month, they arrived at Fukaie-mura, where they chose their position and laid their plans to slaughter the villagers, without letting one man escape.

While thus engaged, about 1,000 of the conspirators, armed with guns, came out; but the soldiers from the castle expecting them, began their fire and shot down more than 20 of the villagers on the spot. The mounted soldiers galloped round, encouraging and commanding the infantry, saying: "This is an affray with farmers and will not amount to much;

---

181 According to "Papinot's Dictionary," the correct name of the Daimyo of Shimabara in 1637 was Matsukura Shigeharu.

just break through at once, and kill all without exception." Thus encouraged, the infantry exerted themselves vigorously to overpower their enemies. But the villagers were a great multitude, and were men accustomed to use the gun in hunting, and moreover were well acquainted with the ground, so that they could quickly pass hither and thither amongst the trees and thickets. They discharged their guns with a certain aim, and shot down on the spot five or six mounted men and about one hundred of the infantry, and thereupon, seeing the dismay of the soldiers from the castle, they grew still bolder, distributed themselves so as to destroy every man, and continued to discharge their balls like rain. As might be expected, the soldiers from the castle could not withstand; and so, collecting into one compact band, they withdrew to the castle of Takaji.

The conspirators followed them, and without delay pushed themselves into the town around the castle, burnt the dwellings of the merchants, and then held a consultation, saying: "The two brothers Matsukura, lords of this castle, are now in Yedo, and there is exceeding small force in it. And more, those who were driven back from Fukaie-mura, being possessed by the spirit of cowardice, can make no defence. Come, let us capture this castle and make it ours, and spend a few days in it in tranquility. And since there are many of our sect in the West, we will not want help. Having committed ourselves to the cause thus, there is no way of escape left. Since, do what we may, our lives are forfeited, let us fight outright; let us make a pillow of this castle." With this, they began the attack on the front gate. The soldiers of the castle under command of Tanaka Sodaiyou and Okamoto Shimbei, assembled before the front gate, and resisted courageously. The conspirators seized spears and long swords, and put handles on sickles and wood cleavers, and with shouts laboured furiously to break in; but the castle had been given to the father of Matsukura Bungo-no-kami Shingemasa as a reward of valour.

It had high walls and ditches and was furnished with towers, and the soldiers of the castle climbed up into the towers, pushed open the portcullises, and discharged balls and arrows.

The conspirators were unprepared to attack and were without armour. More than two hundred were soon shot down and the rest fled in all directions.

CHAPTER III.

Petition for Aid sent from the Castle of Takaji, and the Conspiracy of Miyemura.

In the castle of Takaji there were fifty or sixty mounted men, and not more than seven hundred infantry; and amongst these more than half of the common soldiers were relatives of the conspirators. These kept stealing arms and valuables, and escaping from the castle. Therefore, from the whole number about one hundred were selected and put to death. After this, there were no means at hand for overthrowing the insurgents; all that could be done was to prevent the castle's being taken, and as the conspirators increased in numbers the castle was endangered; hence Tanaka Sodayou and Okamoto Shimbei consulted and agreed to send a messenger for aid to the retainers of Nabeshima Shinano-no-kami Katsushige,[182] lord of the castle of Saga in Hizen, and Hosokawa Echu-no-Kami Tadatoshi,[183] lord of the castle of Kumamoto in Higo.

As both lords resided at that time in Yedo, Kii-no-kami Motoshige and Kai-no-kami Naozumi, sons of Shinano-no-kami,

---

182 Nabeshima Katsushige (1580-1657); his fief was the province of Hizen and his castle town Saga. He took a prominent part in the capture of Hara castle, and was allowed as a special favour to retain the Christian Flag, which is still preserved in the family.

183 Hosokawa Tadatoshi, son of Tadaoki, was baptised at the age of nine but recanted later. His mother was the famous "Gracia" of the Jesuits, who rather than fall alive into the hands of Ishida Kazushige, died by the hand of her husband's retainer at Osaka in 1600.

made Isahayabuzen commander of the forces. He led out more than three thousand men from Saga, and having advanced about six *ri* to a place in the same country (Hizen) called Karita,[184] he encamped. Again, as Echu-no-kami Tadatoshi and his son were both in Yedo, a retainer named Shimizu Hoki,[185] leading more than four thousand men, left Kumamoto and encamped at Kawashiri, in the same country (Higo). But according to the regulation of the government, no one but the appointed officer could go forth to inflict punishment in any country whatever. The matter had first to be referred to the commissioner of the government. Lending aid rashly was calculated to bring one into difficulty; hence the forces of both countries remained in camp, and a messenger was sent to Haiashi Tamba and Makino Denzo, the commissioners for Kiushu, then living in Funai, (Oita), in Bungo. These two men, having heard, sent a messenger to Yedo and sent back word that they would give further orders as soon as instructions came from the seat of government. Thus the aid promised to the castle of Takaji by the two countries was delayed till these instructions were received.

In the meantime the evil conspirators roamed at large and killed without reason those who did not belong to their party; they plundered houses and usurped power over the surrounding country. As many had no love for the Christian sect, in order to escape death they joined it reluctantly, the number soon increasing to eight thousand men. Now, there is a place called Miye-mura, about one *ri* to the North of the castle of Takaji. This was the place where the rice for the castle was usually kept. For the purpose of bringing this rice into the castle, a company of fifteen mounted men, one hundred men armed with guns, and about three hundred infantry, set

---

184 Karita is Karita-no-sho (刈田の庄), the village of Karita.

185 Shimizu Hoki is Shimizu Hoki-no-Kami (志水伯耆守) Shimizu, whose title was Lord of Hoki.

out on the 2nd of the 11th month for Miye-mura.[186] The inhabitants of this place were all Christians. These villagers, several hundred in number, assembled and fired on the soldiers from the castle, and endeavoured to surround and destroy them. These latter also fired in return and resisted, but the conspirators were a great multitude, continually re-inforced, and so prevailed.

The three leaders of the infantry were killed. Besides these, many were killed and wounded, and the rest with difficulty escaped. The rice in Miye-mura fell into the hands of the evil tribe of conspirators, who became more and more insolent and manifested no signs of fear. In the castle of Takaji courage failed ; the defenders gave up all design of attacking, and merely looked for aid from the neighbouring country.

CHAPTER IV.

Insurrection of Christians in Amakusa; Capture of Watanabe Kozaiemon.

There is an island called Amakusa, producing more than forty thousand *kokus** of rice. This island is the property of Terazawa Hiogo-no-Kami Katataka,[187] lord of the castle of Karatsu in Hizen. At a place called Tomioka in this island is a small castle. This had been committed to the care of a man called Miwake Tobei, a retainer of Terazawa, who resided

---

186 Miyemura : This place is mentioned in historical documents relative to the riot of Amakusa under two different Chinese compounds, namely, "三會村" (Miye-mura) and "三江村" (Miye-mura). But, according to modern geography, the former (三會村) seems to be correct.

187 Terazawa Hiogo-no-Kami Katataka 寺澤兵庫頭堅高, son of Terazawa Hirotakaor Masanari. The father was Governor of Nagasaki (1592-1600) ; he fought on the side of Iyeyasu Tokugawa and was rewarded with the Fief of Amakusa besides that of Karatsu, which he had received from Hideyoshi. Katataka, was dispossessed in 1638 after the Shimabara rebellion.

* One *koku*=5 bushels of 36 litres each.

there. There was also a farmer on this island, called Shimbei.[188] He was a Christian, and wandered as far as Nagasaki spreading the doctrines of the corrupt sect. For some years previously he lived in Oodogori, in the above country. His son, Shirodayou, though a youth merely, excelled all men in knowledge and skill. He was not deficient in literary acquirements, and was accomplished in the military arts. He could also perform singular feats. For example, he could call down a flying bird, and cause it to light upon his hand ; could run over the white waves, and the like. As he deluded the farmers by performing various exploits, they unitedly regarded him as a superior being, nothing less than an incarnation of Deus ; and thus they all reverenced him. At that time, Shirodayou, having heard of the insurrection at Shimabara, he and his father together returned to Amakusa, that being his native place. They found out the Christians of like mind with themselves and secretly consulted with them, saying : " The Christians of Shimabara have lately united together and thrown away their bodies and lives for this doctrine. They await the attack of the forces of the Shogun in order to gain their wishes after death. This taking up arms against the government, is, to use an illustration, as if a child should try to measure out the great sea with a shell ; or as if a beetle should lift up its foot to fight against a cart-wheel. Still, when the soldiers of Matsukura Nagato-no-kami attacked them, contrary to expectation, the soldiers were beaten by the insurgents. For farmers to fight with soldiers and gain the victory is a thing unheard of in the past and will be rare in the future. Now, in our opinion, this is not at all owing to the courage of the farmers, but altogether to the aid of Deus. If we do not go to their aid it will be hard to escape the judgment of Heaven. And if we should altogether fail of victory, is it not yet the great desire of our sect to gain Heaven after death ? " They carefully exhorted in this manner,

---

188 Also Jimbei (新兵衛).

and as the hearers were all from the first favourably disposed towards the sect, and fellows who reverenced Shirodayou, they with one mind united with him. They then collected soldiers, kept up communication with the Christians of Shimabara, and resolved to capture some suitable castle and make it their own, and fight intrepidly, resisting the forces of the government; resolved that though their bodies should decay upon the open plain, they would leave their names to future ages, and make their fame resound high as the clouds. About this time, Watanabe Kozaiemon, younger brother of Shimbei and uncle of Shirodayou was Recorder[189] of Amakusa and a leader of the Christians. Shirodayou's mother and his brothers were living in Oodogori still. For the purpose of bringing them to Amakusa, Watanabe, together with four or five intelligent farmers, rowed across in a small boat. Oodogori is in the country belonging to Hosokawa Echu-no-kami. From the time that the rebellion at Shimabara broke out, guards had been placed at all the crossings and landing places to examine travellers. Thus the said Watanabe Kozaiemon was taken alive at Kanoora in Oodogori, and afterwards Shirodayou's mother and brothers were captured, bound and cast into a dungeon.

CHAPTER V.

Petition for Aid from Tomioka to Karatsu.

When the people of Amakusa heard that Watanabe had been captured at Konoora, they perceived that their dark plots were known and that there was no way of escaping

---

189 Recorder. This refers presumably to the office of Chōkata (帳方). Apparently the ancient Japanese Christians, when no longer able to worship openly, formed secret organisations. One member of each community was named Chōkata, or Recorder, being charged with the duty of informing all other members of the dates of Feasts and Obligations; each community also had a mizukata (水方) or person charged with the duty of administering baptism.

Christian Flag captured at Shimabara, and Certificate granted to Nabeshima, the Daimyo of Saga.

with their lives. Hereupon they consulted and resolved that, since they must die, they would wage a wakening war, and die fighting. As a matter of course they did not pay their taxes, being entirely absorbed in their preparations for war. The Governor of the place, hearing this, desired to suppress the disorders ; but, all the people being conspirators, he merely endangered his own person. He hastened to the castle of Tomioka and reported the condition of things. The commander of the castle, Miwake Tobei, was alarmed, and prepared to send troops to the vicinity of Kamitsura to suppress them. Ten mounted men, sixty armed with guns and three hundred infantry, were ready to set out, when news came that the people of Kamitsura, Oyano, Chidzka, Zozoshima, and Yanaginoseto, had all joined the conspiracy, and were courageously preparing to receive and drive back the attacking party. Since this was the case, the castle of Tomioka was clearly endangered, the attacking party was re-called, and hostages were seized in the surrounding villages, confined in Tomioka, and the whole proceedings reported to Karatsu. But Terazawa Hiogo-no-kami was in Yedo at the time, and while his retainers disputed among themselves, days passed away, and the conspirators of Amakusa became more numerous, committed depredations in various directions, killed those who resisted their solicitations, and usurped authority at pleasure ; therefore all yielded to them. Moreover, in Karatsu they continued disputing as to who should go to the aid of Tomioka, so that no conclusion could be reached. Hence they resolved to settle the matter by lot. The lot fell on Okajima Jerozaimon, Okajima Hichirozaimon, Sawaki Hichirobei, and Harada Iyo, and these were made commanders of an army of more than fifteen hundred men. On the 5th of the 11th month they set sail from Karatsu. Though they hastened and were favoured by a fair wind, yet, there being a distance of forty-eight *ri* to sail, they did not arrive at Tomioka in Amakusa till the night of the 7th of the same month. They went on shore from the boats and readjusted the girths of their horses, and prepared to march in the morning to Honto.[190] They presented a very warlike appearance, as if they would stamp the whole evil race of conspirators to death. On the morning of the 8th of the 11th month, soldiers from Karatsu left Tomioka and went to Honto. This Honto is five *ri* distant from Tomioka. The people of Honto and Shimako had, from the very first, united with the Christians of Kamitsura, but the people of Honto informed the soldiers from Karatsu that they (the people of Honto) had been frequently urged by the people of Kamitsura and Shimako to join the conspiracy, but had not yielded ; and owing to their proximity to Tomioka the Christians had not yet attacked them. They also advised them to send one or two hundred troops to Shimako and drive out the Christians, when those of Kamitsura would yield without resistance. This, it is said, was a strategy concocted between them and the people of Kamitsura, for the purpose of decoying some of the people from Karatsu into Shimako and there destroying them.

CHAPTER VI.

Shirodayou of Amakusa made Commander. Battle of Shimako.

The soldiers of Terazawa did not perceive that they were deceived by the conspirators ; and accordingly, on the 9th of the 11th month, Miwake Toemon being leader, he, together with Haiashi Matazaimon, (Hayashi Matsuzaemon) Haiashi Kojuro, Ono Sukezaimon, Kunie Seizaimon, and fifteen or sixteen other mounted men, fifty armed with guns, and more than two hundred common troops, left Honto and came to

---

190 Honto. In Amakusa, there are two villages, one called " Honto " (本戶) and the other " Hondo " (本渡) ; these two village names appear indiscriminately in the Christian documents of Shimabara, so it cannot be told which one is meant by " Honto."

Shimako. As to this Shimako, on the south the mountains are irregular, and the peaks precipitous ; on the north is a wide expanse of sea, from which innumerable waves roll in and break against the shore. On the east and west, the paths were steep and winding, only sufficient for one man at a time. The distance from Shimako to Kamitsura was one *ri** and a half only, while the distance to Honto where the main body was encamped was four *ri*. Also in that distance was more than one *ri* of flooded ground, to cross which the time of the ebb of the tide had to be taken into consideration. There was also a rumour that the conspirators were about to attack a place called Sumotanotachi, and twenty men armed with guns, under the command of Okajima Hichirozaimon and Yamamoto Gorozaimon were sent to its relief, and twenty men armed with guns, under Sawaki Hichirobei, were placed at a guard-house near the land flooded by the tide. The conspirators had already laid their plans to scatter the soldiers from Karatsu, by setting fire to houses in various places, and thus withdrawing companies of twenty or thirty each to various points and render the main body encamped at Honto as weak as possible.

About this time the chief men of the eight thousand conspirators of Shimabara consulted together when one said : " That the soldiers have not gained any advantage over us in the recent conflicts is all owing to the protection which Deus affords us. Still, in the midst of a variety of opinions, it is difficult for us to have unity of action, and unless we elect a commander and obey his commands future success will be endangered. Let us therefore call Oyano Shirodayou and make him our leader." To this all agreed, and sent a messenger to Amakusa and who said to Shirodayou : " Though we recently, at the command of Deus, resolved to risk our lives for our religion, and have revolted against the laws of

* One *ri*=2½ miles.

Japan and taken up arms against the soldiery, we have not yet met with defeat. Is not this because Saint Mary has defended us? Now all our party, to the number of eight thousand, desire you to become their leader, and promise to obey your orders. Come speedily to this place and aid us with your advice." Shirodayou, having heard, replied: "Though I am unworthy of the place, I am already regarded as having the ability of a commander, and five thousand men of Amakusa obey my commands, and are encamped at Oyano and Shikidzu.[191] Your resolution is admirable. To test its truth, I wish to see a paper containing the written oath of the leaders, and of the people, binding themselves to obey me." Thereupon the Christians of Shimabara sent the document to Shirodayou, and he became commander of the villagers of Shimabara numbering thirteen thousand men, and called himself Oyano Shirodayou Tokisada. Shirodayou first went to Fukaie-mura in Shimabara, for purposes of consultation, and a barren and unfrequented island which they named Consultation Island[192] was fixed upon as the place of meeting. When assembled Shirodayou said to them: "The two armies of Shimabara and Amakusa number together thirteen thousand men. Let this number be divided, and one part be stationed at Mogitoge, and one part at Hibitoge, and let messengers be sent to Nagasaki to gather recruits. If there are any who will not yield to the Christians, cut off the head of every one, set fire to their houses, and offer these victims as a sacrifice to the God of War." As those assembled were persons accustomed

191 Shikidzu. This seems to be a mis-reading of the name of the village of "Futsu" (布津): this village is now in the Minami-Takagi-gun of Nagasaki-ken. The character "布" may be read either "fu" or "shiki" or "shiku," but the real name of the village is "Futsumura."

192 Consultation Island. This is identical with the island "Yushima" or "Yujima" (Hot Water Island), situated in the sea between Amakusa-gun of Kumamoto-ken and the Minami-Takagi-gun of Nagasaki-ken. At present there is a village on the island called "Yushima-mura" (湯島村) belonging to Amakusa-gun of Kumamoto-ken.

to obeying Shirodayou, they consented to do this. On the 13th of the 11th month, the conspirators of Kamitsura, having led the forces from Karatsu into Shimako, assembled and planned an attack.

The weather was unfavourable ; still, notwithstanding this, the leader, Oyano Shirodayou, speedily embarked more than five thousand men in small boats, went over to Kamitsura, and sent a party to reconnoitre the position of the forces from Karatsu. These latter were preparing to attack Kamitsura the next morning. The reconnoitering party returned and reported the state of things. Shirodayou, hearing this, said : " It is an old proverb that he who is beforehand controls others, while he who is behindhand is controlled by others. This being the case, we will begin the attack and decide the conflict. With this he distributed his forces ; those from Shimabara were at night to embark in boats and go to Shimako, and attack from the sea-shore ; those from Amakusa were to attack from the hills on the opposite side, both parties to begin the attack suddenly, before daylight. A company of men was selected from the Shimabara army to attack the forces from Karatsu, in case they should give way and retreat towards Honto. The divisions, having received their instructions, set out in the night. The forces from Shimabara were stationed at the landing near Kamitsura under the immediate command of Shirodayou. The forces from Karatsu, while encamped at Shimako, heard that the conspirators at Kamitsura had received reinforcements ; but thought it would not amount to much. They despised their adversaries, regarding them as persons who knew nothing of the art of war, and not to be feared, however numerous they might be. Thus they were unfortunately off their guard. Still, as a kind of precautionary measure, they set some of the villagers to watch on the neighbouring hills. On the morning of the 14th of the 11th month, before the dawn of day, the conspirators began the attack from the land and from the sea. Those villagers who had been set on the look-out, being themselves Christians devoted to the cause of the conspirators, at first led on the assailants in a friendly manner, and afterwards, when sufficiently near, ran forward and gave the alarm. The forces from Karatsu were alarmed; they found the conspirators just before their eyes, advancing close together, bearing innumerable banners made of white linen and white paper, and making an uproar by blowing upon sea shells.

Thus they advanced to the attack. The troops from Karatsu, seizing whatever arms were at hand, went out to meet them. Miwake Toemon, Haiashi Mataemon, Haiashi Kojuro, and Ono Tokezaimon, commanding the troops, resisted bravely, but in vain. The conspirators from Shimabara opened fire from the direction of the sea-shore, while those from Amakusa, to the number of five thousand, advancing from the hills, kept up a heavy fire from the thickets on the east. Thus pressed by the enemy before and behind, ignorant of the way, and unable to advance or retreat, Miwake Toemon ascended a high hill on the south and escaped to a place called Sumoto. Hayashi Mataemon, Haiashi Kojuro, and Ono Tokezaimon, for some time, brandishing their spears, resisted the enemy now near at hand, but at length were struck by balls and killed. After this, the troops from Karatsu scattered to the right and left, and those who thought to escape to Honto were intercepted and killed by the farmers who had been chosen for this purpose. Twenty of the soldiers from Karatsu were killed on the spot, in the battle of the morning. Miwake Toemon escaped from danger, came to Yanagino-Seto and reported that his troops had been defeated at the battle of Shimako, and he came in haste to report the state of things to the troops stationed at Honto. He said that the Christians were innumerable and that it was useless to resist, and without waiting for an answer, hurried on his way. He was hardly gone, when the conspirators also reached Yanagino-Seto. Sawaki Hichirobei defended the place with fifty men and twenty guns.

Sawaki said, as he issued his commands, that Miwake Toemon, pressed by the enemy, had lost his senses, and that hence they appeared strong to him. Let them be even so many as ten thousands, being mere farmers they are not to be feared. So saying, he disposed his men in the thickets, and they shot down some of the foremost of the conspirators; but these last being numerous disregarded this, and advanced, shouting as they came. They quickly killed more than twenty of Sawaki's men, and the rest fled to Honto. Thus the villagers, having gained two victories, advanced immediately upon Honto. In this place Okajima Jirozaimon, Harada Iyo, Ogasawara Saiguske,[193] Sawaki Hichirobei, Miwake Tobei, Miwake Toemon, Tatskuri Hachirobei, Nabika Kuhei, Aoki Kanemon, and Sasa Kozaimon commanded. Okajima Hichirozaimon and Yanamoto Gorozaimon came from Sumoto and joined them. The conspirators, under Shirodayou Tokisada, advanced to the attack, shouting a song of victory. The troops from Karatsu resisted desperately. The mob of conspirators, however, resolved upon death or victory, pressed the attack. Miwake Toemon, Tatskuri Hachirobei, Nabika Kuhei, Aoki Kanemon, and Sasa Kozaimon fought, refused to retreat, and after having killed more than twenty villagers, were themselves killed. The conspirators, though they could have taken the castle of Tomioka on the strength of this success, yet being wearied by three conflicts since daylight, and it being now sunset, encamped in Honto.

193 Ogasawara Saiguske: In the Amakusa Monogatari (The Tales of Amakusa) this person is mentioned as Ogasawara Itsuki-no-suke (小笠原齋之助), while in the Nanto Henran Ki (the Record of Riot of the Southern Island), he is mentioned as Ogasawara Saigu. The "Sai" (齋) in Chinese is pronounced "Itsuki" in Japanese. It is most probable that his family name was Ogasawara and his official title was "Saigu-no-suke," belonging to Saigu-ryo (齋宮寮), in which department official affairs relative to the Ise Shrines are managed, and the "Itsuki-no-suke" may be an abbreviation of "Itsuki-no-miya no suke," which is the Japanese reading of the "Saigu-no-suke." (Saigu=Itsuki-no-miya=齋宮).

CHAPTER VII.

Two Attacks of the Conspirators on the Castle of Tomioka.

Okajima Jirozaimon, Harada Iyo, Miwake Tobei, and thirteen inferior officers, all retainers of Terazawa Hyogo-no-Kami Katataka, commanded in the castle of Tomioka. These having placed their large and small guns in position, awaited the approach of the conspirators. The conspirators, encamped at Honto, held a consultation, and resolved to capture the strong castle of Tomioka, it being unequalled for purposes of defence, and having assembled in it, to carry out their purposes. Shirodayou made preparation to take it by strategy. Accordingly, on the 18th of the 11th month, the Christians, to the number of more than ten thousand, assembled at a place called Shiki, one *ri* from the castle of Tomioka, and there flung several scores of white banners to the wind, and then boldly drew near. The defenders of the castle saw them from a distance. They could not tell the number of the enemy. From the number of white flags fluttering everywhere in the groves and thickets they appeared innumerable.

The soldiers of the castle, fearing a night attack, tied on their armour and prepared their spear-points, and on the morning of the 19th before daylight, more than ten thousand of the conspirators surrounded the castle and began the attack. The soldiers of the castle fired upon them from the loop holes, and more than two hundred of the conspirators were killed in a short time, and the rest withdrew from the attack. Oyano Shirodayou then directed the people to protect themselves with bamboo rods tied in bundles, and ordered them to take doors and use them as shields. The people accordingly tore down the bamboo fences and bound the bamboos in bundles to be used as directed, and on the morning of the 21st of the same month, before daylight, they again approached the castle of Tomioka, shouting as with one voice the following words: "If we die we will ascend to Heaven; if we live we will live in prosperity, and be masters of the castle of Tomioka". Thus, bearing their shields and bundles of bamboos in their hands, they began their attack. The soldiers in the castle met them at the gate, and boldly resisted them. The villagers, though many were cut down and thrust through, would not withdraw, but climbed over the dead bodies, and kept up the attack till the outer wall was taken, and the second wall reached. The leader Shirodayou, waving a white flag, directed the soldiers, who shouted their song of victory, beat drums, and pressed forward to the attack till the second wall also was taken and only the inner wall remained. The conspirators, elated with success, strove to scale this also, and the inner wall appeared to be in danger. The soldiers of the castle stood on the defence, and knowing that should such a castle, guarded by soldiers, however few, be taken by farmers, it would be a disgrace to them to be regretted to future ages, they redoubled their efforts to keep back the assailants. At this juncture Miwake Tobei, commanding in the castle, brought out several hundred fire arrows which he had provided. These, when discharged through the windows, quickly ignited the shields and bamboo bundles of the enemy. A heavy fire from the castle was opened on the farmers, already disconcerted by the fire arrows. Their spirits then fell, and as they were about to give up the attack, their leader, Shirodayou, withdrew them to Karatsu in Shimabara. The villagers of the place afterwards collected in Kamitsura, and the soldiers in Tomioka had a short breathing spell.

CHAPTER VIII.

Arrival of the Imperial Commissioner at Shimabara.

Though speedy messengers were sent, one after another, some by sea in swift vessels, and some on swift horses by land, and though they hastened day and night, the news of the insurrection did not reach Yedo till the 9th day of the 11th month. When this was heard, Doi Oi no Kami, Sakai Sanuki-no-kami, Matsudaira Idzu-no-kami, Abe Bungo-no-kami, and all the wise and experienced counsellors came into the Shogun's presence and carefully informed him of the matter. The Shogun Daiju Iyemitsu[194] summoned Itakura Naizennosho and Ishidani Juzo. Naizennosho, as Imperial Messenger, had charge of the matter, and Juzo was reporter.[195] These two men received their instructions, and on the evening of the same day (the 9th) left Yedo for the west. Both these men secretly believed that though the farmers had rebelled, it would not be a serious matter. They supposed that in consequence of laws in force in the dominions of Matsukura Nagato-no-kami and Terazawa Hyogo-no-kami the people had rebelled, and the name Christian was given to this movement. They lightly thought that the conspirators, when once they should hear of the Imperial Messenger's arrival, would, without fail, come to meet him, and acknowledge their fault. Not only so, but they did not hurry on the way, and so did not reach the castle of Takagi in Hizen till the 30th of the same month. Mondo Shigenori, son of Naizennosho, a youth of twenty-one years, accompanied his father. In consequence of the spread of the insurrection, the princes and their sons who, as before said, resided in Yedo, obtained leave of absence, and returned to

---

194 Iyemitsu was the third Tokugawa Shogun and consolidated the power of that family. "Daizu" is a Chinese classical term applied to a general. Literally, "Great tree."

195 "Juzo was reporter." The original Japanese says "Ometseke" which has been often translated as "spy". The duty of an "Ometseke" was not that of a spy but rather that of an observer to watch how the Government's instructions were being executed. The position of an "Ometseke" with an army may be compared with that of the Dutch Commissioners, who were attached to the Duke of Marlborough in the War of the Spanish Succession (1717) when the Dutch Government allowed that General to have command of the Dutch Army, that is, they observed his conduct of affairs and reported on it to their home Government.

their countries. The reporters, Masano Denzo[196] and Hayashi Tamba, came from Funai, in Bungo. Sakakibara Hida-no-kami and his son came from Nagasaki to Takagi. All these met with the Imperial Messenger, and learned from him the Sovereign's will. Naizennosho and Juzo, having first consulted together, distributed the forces in various places. The troops of Nabeshima Minano-no-kami[197] were sent to Shimabara; those of Arima Gemba-no-kami[198] and Tachibana Hida-no-kami were stationed at the castle of Takagi; and those of Terazawa Hyogo-no-kami and Hosakawa Echu-no-kami, at Amakusa. Other princes, having returned from Yedo, led their troops to Amakusa, whereupon the conspirators, speedily embarking in boats, escaped thence to Shimabara.

CHAPTER IX.

THE CONSPIRATORS FORTIFY THEMSELVES IN AN OLD CASTLE.

Oyano Shirodayou assembled the conspirators and said: "It is known that recently, in consequence of our uprising, the Imperial Commissioner has arrived, and consulted with the princes of the west and will attack us with a great force. It is easily seen that, in our present condition, we will speedily be overthrown by the soldiers. Let us then fortify ourselves in a castle, and wage war as long as we can. We number more than ten thousand men, accustomed to use fire-arms. More than this, as we have resolved to sacrifice our lives for the sake of our religion it is not to be supposed that we will be easily overthrown. What is your opinion?" he inquired. They all agreed to his proposals and selected four of their number to superintend the repairing of an old castle[199] on a

---

196 Masano Denzo: This is for Makino Denzo (牧野傳藏).

197 Nabeshima Minano-no-Kami is for Nabeshima Shinano-no-kami (鍋島信濃守).

198 Arima Gemba-no-kami is for Arima Tamba-no-kami (有馬丹波守).

199 Known to history as Hara Castle. See note 203.

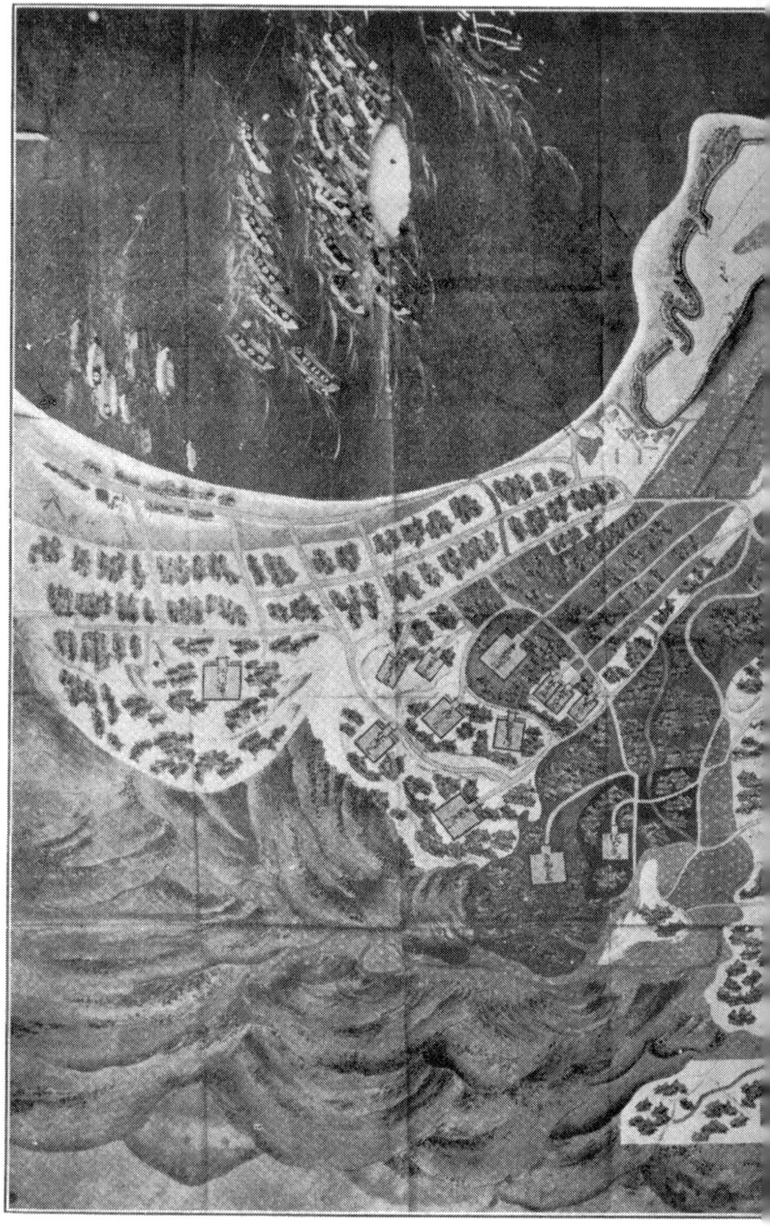

Plan of Hara Castle 1637-1638.

plain in Arima-no-oora. They began work on the first day of the twelfth month, built up the walls and gates, and erected huts. They called the names of the walls as they had formerly been called, namely, the inner, the second and third or outer wall, and took up their respective positions. Oya-no-Shirodayou with two thousand men, defended the inner wall. Five thousand two hundred men defended the second wall, and three thousand five hundred men defended the outer wall. On the 10th day of the 12th month, twenty thousand strong men, besides women and children who swelled the total to more than thirty-seven thousand persons, set up their banners made of white linen and white paper, and prepared to meet the attacking party.

This castle of Hara (Shimabara) was one in which Shirinoske Masadzumi the father of Arima Naozumi had lived for many years. On two sides was the open sea, the waves of which broke against the perpendicular cliffs, rendering it impossible for a boat to land. The tops of the hill were high and steep, and before the castle was a large swamp. The whole circumference was more than one hundred *cho* (about three *ri*, or seven miles). The entire wall was repaired, loop holes cut out, and innumerable banners were set up. These fluttering in the wind, appeared like a white cloud. Though defended by mere farmers, it by no means appeared as if it would be easily taken.

CHAPTER X.

Battle of the 20th of the 12th Month.

The assailants, led by Matsukura Nagato-no-kami, Nabeshima Kii-no-kami, Nabeshima Kai-no-kami, Tachibana Sakontayou, Arima Hyobutayou, assembled before Arima. Then Itakura Naizennosho with the four reporters[200] viewed the castle, after

200 See note page 76.

which they assembled the leaders and said: "When we view the condition of this castle it is not to be supposed that it will be easily taken. If it is taken by storm, many of the assailants will be killed. Let it be surrounded and besieged and thus be taken." Having thus received their orders, the divisions arranged their several encampments. Matsukura Nagato-no-kami occupied the first position. But Tachibana Sakontayou, and Arima Hyobutayou were desirous, both of them, of obtaining this place, and therefore approached near the walls of the castle, and began firing, which was answered as vigorously by those within the walls. Itakura and Ishidani again addressed the leaders, saying: "When we consider the spirit of the assailants, we see that it is useless to spend the time in besieging the place. And more, if this place is not quickly taken, there is no doubt that the villagers in the adjacent countries will rebel; and should the news that the work is not progressing reach the Shogun, he will be displeased. To-night, then, let a shout be raised on all sides, and observe how it affects those within the castle, and then let the place be stormed." Accordingly, that night a shout was raised by all at once, which was answered by a like shout from those within the castle, after which they became quiet and awaited the onset. There being no evidence of disorder within, the assailants desisted from the attack. Then Itakura declared his belief that the place could not be taken except by storm. The next day, the twentieth, was chosen for a united attack. The troops of Nabeshima were to advance to a hill covered with pine on the west and there raise a shout. This was done with the expectation that the farmers would resort to the place. The troops of Tachibana were to approach the eastern entrance secretly, and begin the attack when the shout on the west side was heard. On the morning of the 20th, before daylight, thirteen thousand of Nabeshima's troops, under the command of Isahaya Buzen, ascended the pine-clad hill, on the west, raised a shout and began the attack. But the road here was narrow and crooked, and there was no place for the troops to stand. The assailants thus embarrassed were exposed to a shower of balls from all directions. In a short time several leaders and about two hundred common soldiers were shot down and the rest were withdrawn speedily. Tachibana, who was to attack on the east, led his troops, armed with shields and numbering five thousand men, to their position in the night, where they awaited the appointed signal. When they heard the shout on the west, they shouted in reply, and began the attack. In the castle they had made their regulations, and each one defended his own place, quite regardless of how any other place fared. The place assaulted was defended by Oye Genemon, Futsunoura Kiehza,[201] and Arima Kyuemon, commanding three thousand five hundred men. Each man performed his duty. They shot down those who were at a distance with their guns, and killed those who were near with arrows and stones. When the assailants were ready to give way, a fire was kept up without intermission from three sides upon them, and they rolled back and fell upon those behind them. The killed and wounded could not be counted ; still the leaders encouraged their men and urged them forward. Tachibana Sakontayou, gnashing his teeth, commanded his men to press forward over the walls and take the place ; but in vain. Twelve of his retainers were killed ; twenty-four were wounded with balls, and twenty were wounded with stones. Three hundred and eighty soldiers were killed and wounded. Thirty-four of the followers of the Imperial Commissioners were also killed. Of those in the castle, not one was killed. The assailants now appeared to be discouraged by their failure, and for some time continued to observe the castle from a distance. At this juncture, on the 23rd of the 12th month, a letter fastened to an arrow[202] was shot from the castle. This was picked up

---

201 Futsunoura Kiehza is for Futsu-no-ura Kichizo (布津浦吉茂).

202 Letter fastened to an arrow : This is called "Ya-bumi" 矢文 (Arrow-letters), many of which are extant among various old documents in Japan.

and given to Itakura Naizennosho. In it was written as follows :—" We men, having a common nature and origin, should not be distinguished as noble or ignoble. We are not senseless like trees or stones. Yet we are regarded by you as worthy of reprobation. Though thus regarded we boldly, and unembarrassed by your presence, address this letter to you. In truth, our object is not to become the conquerors and lords of countries great or small; nor is it our object to acquire wealth. We act thus only because our religion is one for which it is difficult to thank Heaven sufficiently. In consequence of the frequent and unrelenting persecutions, and for the sake of the Lord of Heaven, innumerable persons have sacrificed their lives, and left their bodies upon the plains and mountains. Their wives and children have done so also, leaving only their names to posterity. There are no words to describe the condition of persons in our body, half dead and half alive, exposed to shame or punishment, whether innocent or guilty; and we are not soldiers, and have no desire for fame. As we are now situated, though we desire to plead our cause before the Shogun, we cannot do so. This is the time of our people's extreme distress. We have assembled in this castle merely to sacrifice our lives for our religion here, and then depart to the future world. Though we are foolish and blind, we do not forget to desire the future world. Our inevitable fate then is a precious thing. But while we are assembled together and idle in the castle, the aspect of hell is before our eyes. The fierce leaders and soldiers of nine countries array their spear-points against us, threatening to punish the wailing criminals. Already in the castle water is exhausted, and food and fuel are consumed. Troubles increase, and famine is before us. In the present world we must meet the punishment of the sword, but in the future we will, without any doubt, be borne to enjoy the highest rank. Our petition is that our ruler would restrain his anger, entertain a heart of mercy, and forgive the offences of the wives and children of those who have offended you. And if you should give to some ten thousands of them a piece of land then we, though we have cause to resent your conduct, will let you cut off our heads in the castle, and leave our names to posterity. To escape from our present evils and be transformed is our only desire while living or in death. In our distress we desire to make our request known by this letter.

" Addressed with true regard and true reverence.

" 23rd of the 12th Month.

" Let the attendants on the Imperial Commissioner present this to him.

" Within the Castle of Arima."

Now, when the news that the Castle of Hara[203] held out and that the assailants had been repulsed reached the ears of the Shogun, he summoned Ika Mori-no-kami, and after a consultation in secret, Matsudaira Idzu-no-kami and Fujiwara no Oojitetsu received instructions, and left Yedo for the west in the 12th month. News of this event had already been received in the camp at Arima. Ika Mori-no-kami[204] had sent a letter informing Itakura Naizennosho of this fact. Also, Amano Toemon, the messenger of Naizennosho's brother, who was then Governor of Kyoto, brought the same information. Though the particulars were not known, it appeared that, because the attack on the castle did not succeed, a new Imperial

---

203 Castle of Hara: Hara (原) and Shimabara (島原) are two different places. The present Shimabara-machi (島原町) at Minami-Takagi-gun, Nagasaki-ken is the site of the old Shimabara Castle, and the site of the old Hara Castle exists quite near the present Kuchinotsu-mura (口の津村) at Minami-Takagi-gun, Nagasaki-ken; there is some distance between Shimabara and Hara. The Shimabara Castle was sometimes called "Moritake-jo"(森嶽城), while the Hara Castle was often called "Hinoyejo" (日の江城) or "Arimajo" (有馬城), or "Kojo" (古城). The phrase appearing on page 21 "An old castle" seems to be for "Kojo" (古城: old castle).

204 Ika Mori-no-Kami: This seems to be for Mori Iga-no-Kami (毛利伊賀守), as there is no country in Japan called "Mori" (毛利).

Messenger had been appointed and was on the way, and Naizennosho was requested to mature his plans and take the place by storm before his arrival.

CHAPTER XI.

BATTLE OF NEW YEAR'S DAY. DEATH OF ITAKURA NAIZENNOSHO

On the 29th of the 12th month, Itakura Naizennosho and Ishidani Juzo assembled the various leaders and said: "There is a rumour that, since the attack on this castle did not succeed as was expected, Matsudaira Idzu-no-kami has been appointed Imperial Commissioner, and will shortly arrive. If this place is overthrown after his arrival, what face will any one of us have? The attack on the 20th failed from want of agreement amongst our troops. When we look at this castle it is plain that there is no one to help from the outside. Besides, New Year's Day is a day of rejoicing to every man, and hence they will not expect to be attacked. Without doubt they will be off their guard in the castle." So it was resolved to make an attack at 8 o'clock in the morning. Arima Hyobutayou was assigned the first place, and afterwards positions were assigned to the other commanders; whereupon they returned to their respective camps for the purpose of making preparations. On the morning of the 30th of the 12th month, Mondo Shigenori, son of Itakura, said to his father: "You have gained renown already, having distinguished yourself at the two battles of Osaka; as this is my first battle, I desire to precede you to-morrow." Itakura replied: "What you say is true, and your request shall be granted; only be careful of your life, and employ your soldiers—for perhaps I may lose my life in the battle. Arrange your troops beside those of Matsukura Nagato-no-kami. Matsukura is a leader deeply interested in this war, and acquainted with the ground; hence we may expect an unparalleled battle." On New Year's morning Arima Hyobutayou, disregarding the appointed signal in the night, advanced against the outer wall and raised a shout. The other leaders heard the shout, but did not move from their positions. They merely wondered who had violated the regulations by attacking before the time, which had been fixed at 8 o'clock in the morning. The defenders of the castle opened a heavy fire. The soldiers of Arima, disregarding this, and shouting at the top of their voices, laboured to break down the gate. The conspirators exerting themselves to the utmost, discharged their guns, and drove the assailants back, by throwing great stones and pieces of timber upon those who were near. At five o'clock in the morning the assailants were driven back. At this time seventeen leaders were killed, and forty-two were wounded. Of common soldiers, the number of killed and wounded was nine hundred and twelve men. When it was daylight, Itakura Naizennosho went out dressed in black armour, wearing a shaggy looking helmet, and carrying a standard surmounted by a crescent. When it was near the time appointed for the attack, he took an ink box, and wrote the following lines with his own hand, for a memento. "On New Year's Day, last year, in Yedo, I tied on a court-dress hat ; to-day I tie on a helmet, and go out to battle. Thus the world and all things in it change. When the name only remains of the flower which bloomed at the advent of the New Year, remember it as leader of the van." Below this he wrote the words: "Itakura Naizennosho Sigemasa, New Year's Day." Having done this, he immediately went out to the conflict. The time having arrived, the other leaders also advanced, and began the attack on the front gate. Within the castle, Oyano Shirodayou, first of all, and with him men of experience, hastened around the walls, and seeing that the attack was made on one side only, more than two thousand able-bodied villagers, who acted as skirmishers, were sent to the aid of the point attacked. The loop-holes were then opened, and a heavy fire kept up. The assailants replied as vigorously, and the balls flew thick between the contending parties. Those who approached the wall were beaten down with stones; and those who approached still nearer were driven back with spears and long swords. Multitudes of the assailants were slain and the rest retreated in dismay. Here Itakura Naizenno-sho advanced with one company, waving a white banner before his troops, and gnashing his teeth, uttered his commands and reproaches, saying, "Is it for you to come so near and then retreat? Vile fellows, think what kind of an enemy is before you. Is it becoming soldiers to retreat from a small castle defended by a set of farmers, though the place is strong and strongly defended? Return and storm the place." He cried repeatedly, at the top of his voice. But there was a great number, in full retreat, and they did not even hear him, as they went on, tumbling down the hill. Itakura then approached the wall, when a ball struck down his standard bearer. Yoneyama Yokei picked up the standard, and advanced with it. Itakura, brandishing a spear, advanced on a large body of the conspirators. Here his spear was broken; yet he did not desist. The conspirators seized his standard from above and broke the staff in two. Observing also the courageous conduct of Itakura, they concluded that he was the commander, and aimed at him alone. He was soon struck by a ball, which passed from his left to his right side, when he fell instantly and died. Four of his retainers died at the same time, and five were wounded. His son Mondo Shigenori, according to his father's commands, accompanied Matsukura Nagato-no-kami, who was slow in coming forward. Mondo was eager to reach the spot, but owing to the narrowness of the way, and having to make his way through the ranks of Matsukura's troops, he was much retarded. Two of the reporters were wounded. Nineteen of Nagato-no-kami's chief retainers were killed; also nine ronin, and three hundred and fourteen common soldiers. Nabeshima Shinano-no-kami lost, in killed and wounded, two thousand five hundred men in all. Besides these, many of the retainers of the Imperial Commissioners and the reporter were killed. Mondo Shigenori was affected deeply by his father's death, and was prevented from entering the castle by the other leaders. At about 9 o'clock each commander withdrew his troops. It was said that only ninety of the defenders of the castle were killed or wounded.

CHAPTER XII.

ARRIVAL OF MATSUDAIRA IDZU-NO-KAMI. GATHERING OF THE ARMIES OF THE WEST.

When the news that many of the assailants were killed in the battle of New Year's Day, and that Itakura Naizennosho had fallen, reached Kawashiri in Higo, on the 2nd, Hosakawa Higo-no-kami set out with twenty six thousand men, about 2 o'clock the same day, and reached Kawanotsu,[205] about one *ri* from the castle, on the fourth of the same month. The same day, another letter fastened to an arrow, was shot from the castle. In it was written as follows:—

" For the sake of our people we have now resorted to this castle. You will, no doubt, think that for the sake of conquering countries, and acquiring houses, we have done this; but such is, by no means, the case. It is simply because the Christian sect is not tolerated as a distinct sect, as you know. Frequent prohibitions have been published by the Shogun, which have greatly distressed us. Some among us there are who consider the hope of future life as of the highest importance. For these there is no escape. Because they will not change their religion, they incur various kinds of severe punishments, being inhumanly subjected to shame and extreme

---

205 Kawanotsu: according to the Amakusa-Ki (the Amakusa Record), this Kawanotsu (川の津) is for Sugawa-no-ura (洲川の浦), which seems to correspond to the present "Kuchi-no-tsu" (口の津), near the site of the old Hara Castle.

suffering, till at last, for their devotion to the Lord of Heaven they are tortured to death. Others, men of resolution even, solicitous for the sensitive body, and dreading the torture, have, while hiding their grief, obeyed the royal will and recanted. Things continuing in this state, all the people have united in an uprising, in an unaccountable and miraculous manner. Should we continue to live as hitherto, and the above laws not be repealed, we must incur all sorts of punishments hard to be endured ; we must, our bodies being weak and sensitive, sin against the infinite Lord of Heaven ; and from solicitude for our brief lives, incur the loss of what we highly esteem. These things fill us with grief beyond our nature's capacity. Hence we are in our present condition. It is not the result of a corrupt doctrine. 4th of the 1st month of the 15th year of Kanei. Addressed to the attendants on the Imperial Commissioner."

(The translator would here observe that this second letter was sent immediately after the death of the first Imperial Commissioner, in the hope, perhaps, that the cause would fare better in other hands. But it fared alike in both cases. Both Commissioners seemed to think that a Christian had no rights that a Japanese Lord was bound to respect, and could offer no petition that he was bound to listen to, much less, grant. Let the reader now note the cold-blooded manner in which the narrative goes on without an intimation that any notice was taken of either of the petitions.)

Terazawa Hyogo-no-kami, finding that all was quiet at Amakusa, came to Arima on the seventh of the same month. Kuroda Kai-no-kami Nagaoki, and Kuroda Ichino-sho Yukikatsu, leading the soldiers of Fukuoka came to Takagi. Shimadzu Satsuma-no-kami Mitsuhiza, committed his troops to his retainer, Shimadzu Shimotske, who arrived on the 15th. The same month, Matsudaira Idzu-no-kami and Todasamon Ojitetsu arrived before Arima ; the son of Idzu-no-kami accompanying him. When the news that the castle of Hara was well fortified, and would be hard to capture, reached the Shogun, all the daimios of Kiushu received permission to return from Yedo to their dominions. They all arrived before Arima in the early part of the 2nd month, and were assigned to their several positions, all under the control of Matsudaira Idzu-no-kami. In the first place, by the sea side, on the north-east of the castle, Hosokawa Echu-no-kami was stationed, his standard was a two-pronged fork, the prongs wrapped with red cloth. Along with him, his son Higo-no-kami was stationed; his standard was a fork with seven prongs. Together they commanded more than sixteen thousand men.

The whole number of the assailants was one hundred and twenty-five thousand men, under the command of Matsudaira Idzu-no-kami.

CHAPTER XIII.

Traitorous Letter of Yamada Emonsaku.

On the 20th of the 1st month, a letter fastened to an arrow was shot from the castle; it was delivered to Matsudaira Idzu-no-kami, and read as follows:—

"Yamada Emonsaku addresses you with true reverence and respect. I desire to obtain your forgiveness, and restore tranquility to the Empire, by delivering up Shirodayou and his followers to be punished. We find that, in ancient times, famous rulers ruled beneficently, proportioning their rewards to the merit of the receiver, and the punishments to the demerit of the offender. When they departed from this course, for any purpose soever, they were unable to keep the control of their countries. This has been the case with hereditary lords; much more will it be the case with villagers who rebel against the government. How will they escape the judgment of heaven? I have revolved these truths in my mind, and imparted them to the eight hundred men under my command.

These men, from the first, were not sincere Christians; but when the conspiracy first broke out, they were beset by a great multitude, and compelled to support the cause. These eight hundred men all have a sincere respect for the armed class. Therefore, speedily attack the castle, and we having received your answer, without fail, as to time, will make a show of resisting you, but will set fire to the house in the castle and escape to your camp. Only I will run to the house of Shirodayou and make as if all were lost; and having induced him to embark with me in a small boat, will take him alive, bring him to you, and thus manifest to you the sincerity of my intentions. For this purpose I have prepared several boats already, having revolved the matter in my mind from the time I entered the castle. Please give me your approval immediately, and I will overthrow the evil race, give tranquility to the Empire, and, I trust, escape with my own life. I am extremely anxious to receive your orders. Yamada Emonsaku thus addresses you with true regard. 20th of 1st month. To the Commanders of the Royal Army."

Thus it was written, but the writer was one of the leaders of the people, and as it was feared that it might be a strategy to draw the assailants near, and then assault them, no answer was returned. Therefore, Emonsaku once more wrote a letter both in Chinese and Japanese, on sacred paper—(such paper as that on which the names of the gods are written)—and shot it from the castle. After the reception of this, Idzunokami shot back a reply, but Emonsaku knew nothing of this, and the night guard picked it up and delivered it to Shirodayou. Shirodayou, alarmed at this, quickly had Emonsaku arrested, and his wife and children put to death on the spot. Shirodayou and his counsellors, seated in order, made Yamada take his place in the yard before them, when Shirodayou said: "You are a commander within the inner wall, and a leader of the conspirators. For what reason, then, have you sent a treacherous letter to the assailants? Look at the answer," he said, producing it. Yamada replied: "I have never dreamed of doing such a thing. I am indeed known amongst our troops as the commander of eight hundred men. Though I alone might be a traitor, is it probable that all the eight hundred are such? This is, more likely, a plan of the enemy to raise discord in the camp, and secure the destruction of eight hundred men, and thus render the taking of the castle easier. There has been no want of such strategy from of old till now. Hence consider well what you are about to do." Shirodayou replied: "If so, the arrow would have fallen, most likely, at some other place. No doubt, because of a preconcerted signal, it fell at your post. Had it been the design of the enemy to produce discord, they would have taken care to show this letter to others." Yamada replied: "The assailants know where I am posted, and had they shot the letter in at any other point it would have failed of its object. Its falling at my post was well calculated to bring me into suspicion and subject me to examination. But I have no concern for my life. Having deprived me of my family, despatch me also. The future will prove the truth or falsehood of my words." Thus speaking as an honest man, Shirodayou and his counsellors were deceived, and built a prison to keep him in for future trial. Into this Yamada was put. Shirodayou then assembled all the leaders and informed them that, from the contents of the letter, he expected an attack shortly, and enjoined them all to be on the watch. Shiki Tamba and Sumoto Wakyo, with three hundred men, were to move round without intermission day or night.

When food began to become scarce in the castle, the villagers lost their courage. They were like fish in a net; there was no means of escape, and there was no one to deliver them from the outside. Thus they continued looking for an opportunity to escape. But the soldiers of the Princes of Kiushu were encamped around them, as numerous as the blades of grass. If now and then some escaped from the castle they were captured and delivered to Matsudaira Idzu-no-kami, who questioned them as to the interior of the castle. When he asked them if there was a man named Yamada Emonsaku within, they replied that he had been commander of eight hundred men, and a defender of the front wall; but having communication with the assailants and a letter from them having been received, he had been imprisoned at a place called Oeguchi. Thus Idzu-no-kami satisfied himself as to the sincerity of Emonsaku's recantation.

CHAPTER XIV.

Night Attack from the Castle.

Matsudaira Idzu-no-kami summoned the commanders and said: "I have been educated in a peaceful time and have acquired no military renown; still, since I have come hither, commissioned by the Shogun, though my plans may differ from yours, and may appear to you extremely foolish, yet in the matter of taking this castle, follow my instructions. Our recent failure to take the castle was merely because the conspirators stake their lives on its defence. Hence the assailants have frequently been repulsed. This is not an ordinary conflict. In this there is no difference between soldiers and farmers, because firearms are used. In my judgment, since this castle was fitted up in haste, there is no great store of provisions in it. Food will give out in not more than one or two months. From present appearances, when food is exhausted they will try to escape from the castle with eagerness. Should we attempt to take the place by storm there is no doubt that many lives will be lost. Therefore, merely fortify the camp with pickets, and build towers from which to discharge your guns, and when the time to attack comes I will give the word of command." The commanders, hearing this, returned to their respective posts and fortified them with two or three rows of pickets; and built a great number of mounds, and towers ; from which, by frequently discharging their guns, they annoyed the conspirators from a distance. More than fifty junks from Higo and Chikuzen guarded the sea coast, and kept up a fire of heavy guns. Also, by direction of Matsudaira Idzu-no-kami Nobusuna, four or five large ships were called from Nagasaki, the Hollanders,[206] employed to bombard the place ; after which they reconstructed their huts in the castle grounds and built places like cellars in the castle, into which they crowded. These places appear to have been a protection against the bombs. Already the 1st month had passed ; and also the half of the 2nd month ; the landscape, on all sides, was serene, but the villagers in the castle gradually began to be in want of food. They were wearied by the long days, and appeared disheartened, and like caged birds longing after the clouds. Their leader Shirodayou Tokisada called together the heads of the people, and said : " Lately the assailants have ceased to attack the castle, and appear to be waiting till the provisions in the castle are exhausted. Moreover, the provisions in the castle will not last many days ; therefore, the overthrow of this place is at hand,

206 The Dutch were not removed from Hirado to Nagasaki until 1641, so that at the date of the Shimabara Rebellion they were still at the former port. In February, 1838, the Dutch Commercial Resident at Hirado received an order from the Governor of Nagasaki to send, firstly, a supply of guns and ammunition to Arima and, finally, to send two Dutch ships then in Kawachiura, a small harbour near Hirado, to aid in the attack on the Hara Castle. The Dutch have often been severely criticised for assisting in the capture of the Hara Castle, defended as it was, by the Japanese Christians. But it should be remembered that unless Koeckacker had been prepared to risk a massacre of his own people and the complete loss of the Dutch trade, it was impossible for him not to comply. His own story has been published in Volume XI of the Transactions of the Asiatic Society from which we can see how distasteful he found the task. He avoided part compliance by hurrying one of his ships off to Batavia but was forced to appear before Hara with the other, the de Ryp, of twenty guns. He remained only two weeks and effected little, the ground being unsuited to cannon. In March he received sudden notice that his services were no longer required. One Dutchman, named Gillis, was killed by the bursting of a charge.

and we must resolve on some course before our strength is exhausted. What is your advice ? " When he had said this, Ari-iye Kenmots and Baba Nyudo advanced, and said : "Since the beginning of the winter of last year, the soldiers have been on guard day and night, and as they are not made of metal or stone they are, no doubt, wearied. We will attack them in the night and awaken them." Shirodayou replied that it should be so, and added : " When we look at the position defended by Hosokawa, father and son, we see that the troops are numerous and brave. Should we attack this point, many of our troops will be killed. As to the camp of Arima and Tachibana, though their troops appear to be weakened by frequent repulse, the ground is uneven. We will send a force against the camps of Nabeshima, Terazawa and Kuroda, and set fire to the camps, and, with this for a signal, will send a great number of vigorous farmers to the place of conflict, from the castle. These will capture provisions and arms and bring them into the castle, where we all will defy the assailants, however numerous, to take us by force." Having decided upon this course, preparation was made for a night attack. The time fixed upon for the night attack was the 21st of the 2nd month. Watch-words were fixed upon, and more than three thousand men were divided into three bands. Ashidzuka Jubei and Futsumura Daiemon, with one thousand one hundred men, were sent against the camp of Kuroda. Arima Gensatsu, with six hundred men, was sent against the camp of Terazawa. Kotsumura Sampei and Chijiiwa Gorozaimon, with thirteen hundred men, were sent against the camp of Nabeshima. Of these last, five hundred men under the command of Futsumura Sampei, carrying fire-arrows and fire-balls, were chosen to set fire to the camp. These directed their course to the towers. About midnight, Futsumura Sampei and Chijiiwa Gorozaimon silently left the castle and advanced to the camp of Nabeshima, set fire to the towers, and raised a shout, which was replied to from the castle. Nabeshima's troops went out and resisted them bravely. The farmers, too, fought resolutely, the strongest of them having been chosen for the night attack ; but more than a hundred of them being slain on the spot, the rest retreated. Two of Nabeshima's chief retainers were killed and more than twenty wounded. Of common soldiers, one hundred and twenty-four were killed and wounded. The killed, wounded and prisoners, on the part of the farmers, amounted to one hundred and sixty-nine. Also, Arima Gensatsu advanced against the camp of Terazawa, broke through the pickets, and was about to attack the principal tent, when his retainer, Miwake Tobei, brandishing a long sword, met him and encouraged his soldiers to resist. Miwake was conspicuous for his courage, killed three farmers, and received three wounds. Four retainers, who fought alongside of Miwake, were killed, and fourteen common soldiers were killed or wounded. Thirty-three of the conspirators were killed, and three taken alive. Ashidzuka Chubei and Futsumura Daiemon, with one hundred men, advanced against the camp of Kuroda. That night Kuroda Kenmotsu kept watch in the camp of Kuroda. He had placed ten men on guard, near the castle. These returned and gave the alarm, and, at the command of Kenmotsu, bows and guns were brought and arranged behind the pickets, to receive the attacking party. As was expected, they came on like a cloud. Kenmotsu twice led on his men and drove the enemy back ; but the third time he was shot through the helmet and died. His son, Okada Tsukezaimon, bearing a torch, seeing his father's death, rushed as he was into the midst of the conspirators. After him, Ogawa Nuinosuke and Suge Kambei, with sixteen retainers and the soldiers of the two sons of Kuroda, advanced with shouts, and when ninety of the villagers were killed, and seven taken alive, the rest fled in various directions. Nine retainers of Kuroda were killed or wounded. Of common soldiers, one hundred and seventy-four were killed or wounded. One retainer of his son, Kuroda Kai-no-kami, was killed, and eleven wounded. Twenty retainers of his other son, Kuroda Ichinosho, were killed or wounded, and of common soldiers, fifty-three. The soldiers of Tachibana, whose camp was alongside that of Matsukura, went out and captured three of the conspirators. After this, strict guard was kept.

CHAPTER XV.

Battle of the 27th of the 2nd Month.

The assailants repaired their towers and pickets, which had been destroyed in the night attack, and continued to discharge their guns from a distance, and kept up a strict watch. The Daimios of the various countries, for the purpose of observing the state of things before Arima, sent one or two retainers, with five or ten common soldiers each. Also the Ronin, from all parts, for the purpose of securing employment under the Daimios, set out for the same place. After the wars of Keicho and Genwa (from 1596 to 1623), the whole country was united under one government, the arrow had been put in its quiver, and both soldiers and farmers lived in tranquility, congratulating themselves on their good fortune, when suddenly this rebellion arose, and took them by surprise. Then all kinds of armour were well made and highly ornamented. Nabeshima Shinano-no-kami, one day, faced the castle, and having surveyed it well, called his retainers, and said to them: "When we look at the part of the castle opposite us, it appears that the inmates of the castle have ceased to pass by there. This is because of the heavy fire kept up on this part from the mounds and towers. Let us then take the first wall, erect pickets, and keep up a fire. If we do so, the farmers, unable to endure it, will certainly come out, and attack our camp; and we, then, will drive them back, and, entering along with them, take the castle." Thus he commanded. The time fixed was noon of the 27th. When the troop left the camp of Nabeshima and approached the wall, the other divisions, engaged in the siege, seeing this, suspected that Nabeshima was preparing to violate some of the regulations. But Nabeshima's men replied to their inquiries that such was not the case—that being near the wall, it was necessary to use precautions. So no one complained. Nabeshima then placed three hundred men, in armour, behind the pickets, for the purpose of repelling any attack that might be made from the castle. The inmates of the castle saw that Nabeshima drew near, and, when they attempted to drive him back, his soldiers, under the command of Isahaya Buzen, opened a heavy fire upon them, and the villagers were disconcerted thereby. At this juncture, Saiemon Norinobu,[207] a youth of seventeen, son of the inspector, Sakakibara Hida-no-kami, taking with him seven or eight men, ascended the second wall, and raised the cry that the first to ascend the castle was Saiemon Norinobu. His father Hida-no-kami, seeing this from a distance, perceived that the man on the second wall, bearing a yellow standard, was his son; and straightway began to ascend the wall also. Nabeshima, seizing a white standard, gave the word of command, knowing that it would be a shame to let the inspector and his son be hurt; and with them Shinano-no-kami, Kii-no-kami and Kai-no-kami, leading a great army, at once rushed in; when a ronin called Fujida Hichibee, of Saiemon's company, set fire to the gate. The various divisions, seeing this, knew that Nabeshima had made an independent assault, whereupon all seized their arms, and rushed forward. Nabeshima assaulted the gate of the 2nd wall, and laboured to break it down at once; but, as this was an important place, the conspirators defended it well; and much time was here lost. Hosokawa Echu-no-kami and Hosokawa Higo-no-kami attacked on the side next the sea, broke down the gate and cut down the Christians, everyone, and having broken down the outer wall, also, at the same time forced their way within the second wall. It is said that when Hosokawa, father and

207 Saiemon Norinobu is for Sakakibara Saemon-no-suke Norinobu (榊原左衛門佐教信): Saemon-no-suke was his official title.

son, entered from the sea side, a number of the farmers had gone out to gather seaweed. There were two or three hundred of these, and many of them were killed as they tried to escape into the castle. The pursuers entered along with the survivors, and took possession of a corner of the central castle, which they fortified. The assailants fought alongside the central wall. Hosokawa and his son desired to capture the central position that day, but a heavy fire was kept up from the wall, and great stones and pieces of timber were hurled upon their troops, so that after having lost a great number, they withdrew. Nabeshima also continued the conflict, but the sun having gone down, the commanders encamped on the ground, and prepared to take the central position in the morning. That night Kuroda Emonnotske called his followers, and said: "Everyone knows the disadvantages under which we have laboured to-day, and that we could not have done better than we did. Still, it is a matter of grief to me that we were behind the others in storming the walls. The time to begin the attack is fixed at 8 o'clock to-morrow morning; but we will begin the attack before daylight, and be the first to mount the inner wall. Let this order be circulated in our camp, and let preparation be made accordingly." Having said this, his retainer, Kuroda Mimasaku, advanced, and said: "As you have truly observed, our position was full of difficulties. Still, to be surpassed by Nabeshima and Hosokawa will render us contemptible and liable to be reproved by the Shogun. This must not be. To-morrow morning, I, though I am old, will go foremost, and to repay the debt of gratitude which I owe my master, will leave my old bones upon the walls of this castle." Hearing this, Kuroda Emonnotske was moved to tears, and replied: "You have always been faithful, but your present fidelity is something extraordinary, so I will assign to you and your son the first place." Also, Itakura Mondo presented himself before Ishidani-Juzo, and said: "My father, Naizennosho, was killed by the conspirators. Though I am not ambitious to gain renown by fighting with farmers, I would like to lead my father's troops to-morrow to the conflict within the castle." Ishidani hearing, consented, advising him to take care of his valuable life, and promising to follow after him.

CHAPTER XVI.

Fall of the Central Portion of the Castle, and the Massacre that Followed.

About six o'clock on the morning of the 28th of the 2nd month, Kuroda Emonnotske, Kuroda Kai-no-kami and Kuroda Ichi-no-sho, attacked the central wall, Kuroda Mimasaku in the first place. This castle was very strong, the stone wall high and steep ; but as Kuroda's troops had resolved to lose their lives in the attempt, they began the ascent with shouts. The inmates of the castle, knowing that that day's fight would be the last, resisted, hurling down great stones and timbers. Multitudes were crushed and killed, but Kuroda's troops would not retreat ; they continued to scale the wall, and at last entered. Thus Kuroda Emonnotske was the first to enter within the central wall. Thereupon the assailants from all quarters advanced, with shouts, to the attack. Several hundred fire-arrows were discharged by Hosokawa's troops. These ignited the house of Shirodayou Tokisada, and soon the black smoke ascended to the sky. Hereupon all the Daimios, together with the messengers from the various countries, and the ronin, rushed eagerly forward. Itakura-Mondo entered the castle at the point which had been captured the day before by Hosokawa's troops, where his way was stopped. Having explained his object to the commander of that place, the pickets were broken down, and Mondo was allowed to pass through. Mondo entered the castle rejoicing. He was a youth of twenty-two years, clad in red armour and armed with a spear. With four followers beside him, he attacked the farmers, piercing many of them through. The whole body of the assailants entered along with him. The villagers fought with desperation, as those whose life was limited to the present moment. They resisted, hurling stones and timbers upon their enemies. The assailants drove them into corners, and cut them down or pierced them through, and took their heads, while their bodies were left piled one upon another. Oya Shirodayou Tokisada, who had been chosen leader of the Christians, was killed by Gintskezaimon, a retainer of Hosokawa. By noon of the 28th of the 2nd month, of Christians who had assemble in the castle, old and young, men and women, more than thirty-seven thousand persons, were destroyed; the place was filled with dead bodies, in heaps, and the blood flowed in red streams. When we count the killed and wounded of the assailants in this fight and that of the day before, we find that Hosokawa and his son lost 274 killed and 1,826 wounded; Kuroda Emonnotske lost 213 killed and 1,657 wounded; Kuroda Kai-no-kami lost 32 killed and 345 wounded; Kuroda Ichinosho lost 16 killed and 156 wounded; Nabeshima and his two sons lost 160 killed and 683 wounded; Tachibana and his son lost 127 killed and 379 wounded; Arima and his son lost 78 killed and 185 wounded; the brother Katsukura lost 27 killed and 97 wounded; Ogasawara Shinano-no-kami lost 25 killed and 203 wounded; Ogasawara Okyo-no-daibu lost 19 killed and 148 wounded; Matsudaira Tago-no-kami lost 31 killed and 128 wounded; Midzuno Hyogo-no-kami 108 killed and 382 wounded; Terazawa Hyogo-no-kami 23 killed and 35 wounded; Arima Saimonnotske and his son lost 39 killed and 301 wounded; Todasamon lost 4 killed and 34 wounded; Matsudaira Idzu-no-kami and his son lost 6 killed and 186 wounded; besides these many others were killed and wounded. One hundred and five of the conspirators were taken alive. Yamada Emonsaku, who had sent the letter on the 20th of the previous month, was brought out of his prison, and having been examined, was confined in the camp of Matsudaira

Idzu-no-kami. Idzu-no-kami and Todasamon Ogitetsu then left Shimabara and went to Amakusa and Nagasaki, and completed the regulations. The heads of the conspirators were buried under a mound at the entrance of a street in the port of Nagasaki. After this, they went to Fukuoka, in Chikuzen ; and then, in the early part of the 4th month, they went to Kokura, in Buzen. At that time, Ota Bitchu-no-kami, commissioner from the Shogun, arrived at Kokura. Having consulted with Idzu-no-kami and Todasamon, they together resolved to assemble the various commanders and make known to them the royal will. Then it was decreed that Matsukura Nagato-no-kami, since the rebellion at Amakusa and Shimabara resulted from his bad government, for which he deserved death, should have this penalty relaxed, and merely be committed to the keeping of Morinaiki Minamoto-no-Nagatsugu, because he had distinguished himself by his bravery during the war. His son, O-okon Katsushige, was banished to the country of Sanuki, and committed to the keeping of Ikoma Sanuki-no-kami. (Others say that Matsukura Nagato-no-kami was committed to Arima Gemba-no-kami, and his son, O-okon, to Hoshina Higo-no-kami.) Terazawa Hyogo-no-kami was in the same condemnation ; but, because he risked his life in taking the castle, as the Shogun heard, his territory of Amakusa, yielding 40,000 *kokus*, was confiscated merely. Nabeshima Shinano-no-kami, Sakakibara Hida-no-kami and Saiemon Norinobu, having attacked the castle before the appointed time, incurred the Shogun's displeasure, but were shortly afterwards received back into favour. The castle of Takagi, the residence of Matsukura, was committed to the care of Ogasawara Iki-no-kami and Goto Awaji-no-kami. The commissioners then returned to Yedo. The castle of Takagi was then given to Koriki Setsu-no-kami. He entered it in the 15th year of Kanei (1638) and governed it with rigour.

PART III

With the defeat of the Christian rebels at Shimabara Christianity in Japan received a deadly blow. All further leniency ceased. The Portuguese merchants at Nagasaki who, despite the persecution, had received consideration, were restricted to the Island of Deshima, and when it was found that this precaution did not prevent them introducing foreign priests the final decision was taken to sever all relations with foreigners other than the Chinese and Dutch. In 1639 all the Portugese, including their wives and their children, were deported[208] to Macao and from that year until 1873 things Christian were forbidden under pain of death. The persecution became more intense than ever, neither men, women or children being spared. The most horrible cruelties were practiced to secure apostates, for the authorities desired by this means to mock Christianity. But, as the long lists of martyrs show, many were steadfast and preferred death to recantation. Helpless, however, the great bulk of the Japanese Christians forsook their religion, at least outwardly, for that of their forefathers. The last foreign priest to set foot in Japan was the Italian Father Sidotti in 1707 ; he was quickly captured and interned at the so-called Christian Yashiki or Mansion in Yedo (Tokyo) where he died in 1715, executions by this time having almost ceased. Suspected Christians were still imprisoned but only in isolated cases were extreme measures taken, the authorities being apparently satisfied that the " evil sect " had been stamped out. But this was not so. On the re-opening of the country the first Roman Catholic Fathers to return searched at first in vain for any trace of the lost Christians. Some inkling that they existed was obtained in 1857 when a Russian Priest ashore from his vessel at Shimoda was accosted by a Japanese farmer, who announced

208 Relations with Manila and Mexico had ceased in 1624, both Japanese and Spaniards forbidding intercourse.

himself as a Christian. He was taken on board and subsequently to Russia. But it was not until 1865 that surmise became certainty. Since 1863 Catholic Priests had been at work again in Nagasaki and its neighbourhood, once the heart of Christianity in Japan. Father Petitjean, later Bishop of Nagasaki, has left an account of his discovery of the descendants of the ancient Japanese Christians :—

" On Friday, March 17th," says he, " towards 12.30 p.m. a group of some twelve to fifteen men, women and children were standing in front of the newly-erected Church of the Twenty Six Martyrs. Their behaviour denoted more than curiosity. I was certainly inspired by my Guardian Angel to go and see them. The door of the Church had been shut. I opened it ; then, followed by my visitors and calling upon them God's Blessing, I proceeded towards the sanctuary. When I arrived before the Tabernacle I knelt down and adored our Lord Jesus Christ in the Holy Eucharist. I worshipped Him and earnestly begged Him to vouchsafe on my lips the words that might touch my hearers and gain some of them to his Love. But I had scarcely been praying the time of an Our Father when three women, aged from about 50 to 60 years, came and knelt near me ; and then one of them, placing her hand on her heart, said to me in a whisper, as if fearing the walls might betray her words :

" ' The heart of all those present is the same as yours '.

" ' Indeed ', I replied, ' but from where do you come ? '

" ' We are all from Urakami. At Urakami nearly all have the same heart as we have.'

" And the woman asked again: ' Where is the Figure of the Virgin Mary ? ' On hearing this name I doubted no more that I was in the presence of the ancient Japanese Christians."

But hardly had these lost children been restored to the bosom of the Church when a second persecution bid fair to rob her of them again. The Japanese authorities had not been unmindful of the past. This is clear from the translation,

The modern Roman Catholic Church at Urakami, commonly called Urakami Cathedral.

which follows, of a Japanese pamphlet written soon after the opening of the country and before 1868, when it was found and translated by Mr. Russell Robertson, then British Vice-Consul at Osaka.

Once more there is seen the same overwhelming dread of conquest by religion, proving that this traditional belief still lingered in the minds of the officials. The writer of this pamphlet is unknown, but the people to whom it is addressed are emphatically warned that to believe in Christ is incompatible with loyalty to the State. It is probable that the author was one of the officials who visited Nagasaki after the discovery of the Christians, sent thither to defend the land from this unexpected menace.

But this time the Christians had, if not defenders, at least spokesmen, and the Foreign Consuls took up their case vigorously as is shown in the correspondence printed after the pamphlet entitled " Gossip about the Rise and Progress of the False Religion in Nagasaki." The most interesting among these will be found to be a report to the British Minister regarding an interview had with the famous Kido Junichiro, later known as Kido Takamasa or Kido Koin.* He, as the Consul's report shows, fully shared the views of Japanese officialdom in the seventeenth century. But fortunately he went abroad in 1872 with Prince Iwakura, and it was not long before he became convinced that his opinion had been erroneous. Sent at first into exile as ordered by the Mikado's Proclamation, translated hereafter, the Christians were recalled in 1873 and allowed to return to their homes free to exercise their religion untrammelled by Government interference.

Gossip about the Rise and Progress of the False Religion in Nagasaki.

The Roman Catholic Religion.

A Roman Catholic Chapel has been erected by Frenchmen at Oura in Nagasaki and some five or six priests have come

* He afterwards became Minister of Education.

and taken up their residence there. They employ some twenty native men of letters, paying them 100 to 200 Rios per annum, and equipping them either as merchants or pilgrims, send them to the following places in Hizen, *viz*, Hirado, Shimabara, Fukahori, Amakusa and other places,[209] where they make converts either by giving money to the poor, by performing miracles to those who love wonders, or by appealing to the passions of people, so that immediately some one or two hundred people are converted who no longer obey the Lord of the soil and even go so far as to disregard all the social amenities of mankind—a fearful state of things indeed.

A certain spy once going to the village of Urakami and concealing himself under the verandah of a house heard a priest of the false religion expounding as follows: Those that become of my faith and believe in what I preach will ascend to Heaven and enjoy everlasting happiness—the followers of Buddhism and Shintoism will be cast into hell, and be in everlasting misery; if one of the family embraces my faith, by his good work alone, all will ascend to Heaven.

After this, in the midst of a ray of glorious light, a magnificent lofty palace appeared, and lovely beings were seen in sweet communion together—consequently the wish to die and go to these Heavenly places has taken hold on the hearts of the men to such an extent that they fear no punishment.

Note:—In another part I will note down many other of the wonderful things.

---

209 Hirado, Shimabara, Fukahori and Amakusa were all ancient centres of Christianity besides Nagasaki with its outlying villages of Urakami and Mogi. At Urakami to-day there is a Cathedral capable of sitting four thousand people, showing to what extent Roman Catholicism has regained its hold in Japan. At the residence of the Priest in charge may be seen a small Museum consisting of relics, medals, books, images, etc., preserved by believers during the centuries when they were cut off from all spiritual guidance of Catholic Priests. Dr. Nagayama, the Librarian of Nagasaki Prefectural Library, has published a book "Collection of Historical Materials" containing many pictures dealing with the story of Christianity in Japan.

The Protestant Religion.

At Oura in the same place (Nagasaki) Americans and English have erected a Protestant Church, and five or six priests have come who lay themselves out to deceive the wise and illustrious men of our glorious country.

The Professors of this Protestant religion live for the most part in native houses, and outwardly appear to teach Astronomy, Geography, Artillery, Medicine etc., but really are all the time desirous of instilling the poison of the false religion.

On comparing the two religions, the Protestant is by far the worst—it sounds all very well at first hearing, but you find at length that it holds the same fox[210] as the other—and does much more mischief.

The mode of speaking adopted by its professors is as follows :

" The Protestant Religion that I advocate does not profess to work miracles, but sets forth the observance of the true human relations as constituting the happiness of the Empire—now look at these books "—and he converts by showing them such books with high sounding titles as Shin ri ichi,[211] Gorin sastu yô,[212] So jô Sastu yô,[213] tells them to throw over their false gods, and in the matter of disrespect to master and parent differs in no way from the principles of the Roman Catholic faith—for all these reasons dire in its effects on the country.

Shoshiso,[214] a Chinaman, writing to a friend of mine says : I have gradually become intimate with the retainers of different

210 Fox. The Japanese are very superstitious regarding the Fox which can, it is believed, bewitch anybody. Inari Shrines or Fox Temples are common where people go to propitiate by prayer and gifts the deity to save them from bewitchment.

211 Shin ri ichi (Ran ?) 眞理一 (覽 ?), Birds' eye View of Truth.

212 Gorin Satsu Yo (五倫撮要), Compendium of the Five Human Relations.

213 So (Shu ?) Jo Sastu Yo (衆生撮要), Compendium of Human Beings.

214 Shoshiso (諸思想), Various Thoughts.

Daimios resident in Nagasaki. One and the other have told me that they had come to Nagasaki at the orders of their respective chiefs to pursue Foreign Studies. As a rule foreigners live by bloodshed ; Astronomy, Geography, weapons of war and nicknacks afford pleasure to the ear and to the eye, but in all their books there is not one that does not sound the praise of God and Christ—and those that read these books, unless they read them in all singleness of purpose and with one object, they will unconsciously come to entertain a respect for these doctrines. My fear is that in two or three years the Roman Catholic and Protestant faiths will be established throughout Japan.

These remarks are only too true. If it comes to this, the people will thus be made the enemies of their own country by foreigners. On my knees I pray that good and noble men will not be led away by these false and corrupt doctrines, and that they will by every principle of honour restrain others and use every endeavour to keep the country firm as a rock in its established faith.

The Substance Of the Corrupt Religion.

The source of the Roman Catholic and Protestant Religion is the same, and they only differ by flowing in different streams. Three hundred and fifty years ago a priest of the Roman Catholic religion[215] headed a particular sect which, professing the true faith of Christ, was called the Christian Religion (Protestant).

The form of the Roman Catholic Religion is to worship wooden images and to perform miracles—the form of the Protestant is not to worship pictures or images of Christ but simply to expound its doctrines, and apparently does not perform miracles ; it makes the Old and New Testaments the basis of its doctrines. In the beginning of the Old Testament it states that 5868 years ago God made the heavens and the earth, the sun, moon, stars, vegetation, birds and beasts, in five

215 Refers to Martin Luther.

days ; on the 6th day He made the first man and woman, the parents of all mankind, who became man and wife—for this reason God is called the Creator, also Lord of all, and Our Father—and by this reasoning one's own master and parents become secondary in importance, which entirely upsets the doctrine contained in the verses of Confucius that " there is no place under the broad expanse of Heaven which is not the King's territory, and the King's Subjects are in all Corners of the Earth".

Again, the reasoning that the bodies of mankind are formed from the Earth made by God, and that life itself is the gift of God, upsets the Confucian doctrine that one's body with its hair and skin is derived from one's parents. To sum up, Lord and parents are regarded merely as the nurses that nourish the body. Again, the sacrificing to ancestors is said to be a thing hateful to God, thus treating lightly what is due to Lord and parents, and setting aside *in toto* the duty of servant to master, of child to parent—truly a great misfortune for the country.

In the Old Testament are what are called the 10 Commandments of God. In the first it is written—" Thou shalt have no other Gods but me "—consequently the apostates in Urakami have either burnt, thrown into the water or pitched into the waterclosets the sacred fuda, (tablets), of Tensho-ko-daijin, Kasuga Daimiojin and Hachiman Daimiojin.[216]

The 6th Commandment says : Thou shalt not kill. But this only applies to the killing of those of the same religion ; if there is any one who does not believe in their faith, however talented or brave he may be, he is put to death. In the 7th : Thou shalt not commit adultery—but

216 Tensho-ko-daijin (天照大神) meaning Amaterasu Ō Mikami or the Goddess of the Sun.

Kasuga Daimiojin (春日大明神) or Ame-no-koyane-no-mikoto (天兒屋根命).

About Hachiman Daimiojin (八幡大明神) there are various theories among students as to this deity, but it is commonly believed that it is the deified Ōjin Tenno.

there are in the Old Testament many instances of father and child, brother and sister cohabiting and yet receiving favours from God—and even now at Urakami and other places there are what are called friendly meetings which consist in men and women meeting secretly late at night and committing adultery. In the 8th: Thou shalt not steal—but is not the stealing of and holding in subjection other countries the greatest of thefts?

Again, in the New Testament an account is given of the life of Christ from his birth to his crucifixion. He first led a life of great poverty—at the age of fifteen he went to a foreign country and, travelling through different regions, learnt many wonderful things, cured men's diseases, stilled the raging of waters, and did other wonderful things, taking in weak-minded people and making them his disciples—but his diabolical plot to assassinate the King of Judea and win over his people and country becoming known he was crucified and put to death—a most horrible criminal. In this it is said that in suffering crucifixion he took upon himself the sins of the people. Again it is written that after his death he came out of his grave and for 40 days explained the scriptures to his disciples, and that at the expiration of the 40 days he was taken up alive to Heaven, but this is a thing that exists only in the minds of his disciples and is altogether without foundation. A religion having for its source such villainous deeds is not likely to number among its followers men of fidelity and filial piety—look at the examples it sets—that however unfaithful or unfilial to master or parent, only love God and you will attain to Heaven.

What took place at Shimabara and Amakusa has had a bad effect. Alas—men nowadays are so eager for novelty.

Since the autumn of last year only, in consequence of fudas, images, and all sorts of things raining from Heaven people in town and country have been holding festivals, dancing with frenzied excitement, bawling out songs in their drunkenness, and foregetting themselves in many ways. If they allow themselves to be beguiled by these false and corrupt doctrines (Roman Catholic and Protestant Religion) misfortunes will undoubtedly fall on the country. Let those in Japan who think at all on this subject acquaint themselves fully how these doctrines militate against every law of fidelity of filial piety, mark how its real spirit is that of converting Japan, and by every law of honour restrain the hearts of men so that these false and corrupt doctrines may not enter in through a single crevice. I call upon every one to do what he can in howsoever small a degree, in this good work.

This is not written for the instruction of the general run of men, but as an exponent of my honest ideas on the subject, and as food for gossip with young people.

Particulars About the Corrupt Religions in Nagasaki.

Since the opening of Nagasaki to foreign trade, amongst the foreigners residing there Frenchmen have been most prominent in disseminating the Roman Catholic religion, Americans and Engilish in disseminating the Protestant. In addition to these two creeds are the Greek Church, the Mahommedan and various others, but their doctrines are all derived from one source and are alike mischievous in their effects on a country.

There is a Roman Catholic and Protestant Church in Nagasaki, and both secretly make converts among the Japanese.

The Roman Catholic converts men of the middle and lower classes, while the Protestants for the most part are men of the middle and upper classes.

The spread of the Roman Catholic Religion may be judged by the following.

In Urakami ... ...Over 2,000 converts.
On the Omura estates... ... ...Over 100 „
Fukabori in Hizen ... ...Over 1,500 „

In Takahama, Shimabara, Amakusa, Hirado, every day fresh converts are being made, and it is not known exactly to what numbers they have attained.

Owing to the apostacy existing in Urakami, a number of the inhabitants were seized by order of the Governor on the evening of the 13th of 6th month last year and cast into prison. On that occasion the images etc. in the Chapel at Urakami were confiscated and put in charge of the Mayor. The policemen returned with seventy men to the Governor's residence. Six or seven, however, remaining on duty at the Mayor's house in Urakami, the remainder of the apostates—some hundreds—raised an outbreak and made an attack with bamboo spears etc., on the Mayor's house, retook their images and made prisoners of two Yakunins and two policemen whom they declared they would hold as hostage and not give up until their companions who had been put in prison were restored to them. In this position of affairs the remainder of the apostates were left to themselves and the arrests ceased. On the 14th a large prison was hastily run up at Kojima, and the above 70 and odd prisoners placed in it. The inhabitants of Nishi, a neighbouring village to Urakami, firm in their original faith and strict in their fidelity and observance of filial duty, although contiguous to Urakami, had not a single apostate among them. On the occasion of the seizures in Urakami the Yakunins were a good deal frightened, and would not set foot among them, but the Nishi people, knowing that it was an occasion to show their loyalty, went right in among the enemy and did capital work. There also being apostates on the Omura estates situated in Urakami, in the 7th month of last year upwards of 100 of them were arrested and cast into prison; those arrested and imprisoned by order of the Governor were summoned daily and the evils of the corrupt religion laid before them, but to no purpose. Firm in their obstinacy, they exhibited no sign of changing their ideas, but on the contrary begged to the allowed the free and unrestricted exercise of the Roman Catholic Religion.

In this posture of affairs, and the Governor and Daikwan[217] not knowing what to do—on the 14th of the 8th month the priests of the seven temples of Shinshu, and of the two temples of Zenshu[218] (nine temples in all) were hastily summoned by the Governor, and on presenting themselves were asked if there was no way of making these Apostates in Urakami change their ideas. The priests left saying that they would make their reply after giving the subject their best attention. On the following day the priests said that they would use their best endeavours to make them change their ideas at once.

On the 19th the Daikwan and Magistrates accompanied the Priests to Urakami ; but notwithstanding all their exhortations they (the apostates), stubborn to a degree, would not pay the least attention, their obstinacy being all due to the leniency with which they had up till now been treated.

In the middle of the 9th month, those imprisoned by the Governor, feigning to change their opinions, were set at liberty, but they again broke out, and their numbers increased daily.

Those that were released were simply given over in charge at Urakami and nothing more. Taking advantage of the leniency with which they had been treated, they took a lot of money from the Chapel, went secretly in all directions, and made converts either by bestowing alms on the poor or by performing miracles, so that within a short space of time hundreds of converts were made in different places.

In the 4th Commandment of the false religion it is written "Thou shalt keep a day of rest." By degrees Japanese having come to observe this day, make it appear as if they had been converted to these doctrines.

The Roman Catholic Religion having spread to such an extent as noted above, endeavours are also being made to disseminate the Protestant religion, and in this view Maria the

---

217 Daikwan (代官) *i.e.* Magistrate.

218 Temples of the Shin sect and Zen sect (真宗寺院, 禅宗寺院).

wife of the Protestant priest Verbeck,[219] leaving the infant at her breast, has gone to Shanghai and Hongkong to return with several priests to Japan.

This is a general outline of the apostacy existing in Nagasaki.

Not much is known with regard to Yokohama and Hakodate, but as several priests reside in both these places, Japanese will without doubt gradually come to be converted.

As Hiogo has been opened to Foreign trade since last winter, and in the event of priests arriving—within a short interval of time the insidious poison will reach to Kioto and Osaka—alas, how lamentable a prospect, while they have not yet laid hands on any one, let some plan be hit upon to prevent the introduction of this false religion.

Among the apostates in Nagasaki there are some so earnest in their faith that they will in no way change their ideas. I think a severe example should be made of these—with regard to those who are lukewarm in their belief, I am of opinion that if some means were adopted by which they might be reasoned with, they would return to their original faith.

The above is a general summary of the spread of the false religion.

[Translated by RUSSELL ROBERTSON.[220]]

June 25th 1868.

219 Dr. Verbeck was one of the first American missionaries to arrive after the re-opening of the country; he lived at first at Nagasaki but moved later to Tokyo, where he was taken into the service of the Japanese Department of Education.

220 Mr. Robertson was British Vice-Consul at Osaka in 1868.

Reports
by H.B.M. Consul at Nagasaki
on the Second Christian Persecution 1868.

Nagasaki, May 14th, 1868.

Rumours have been in circulation for several days regarding the persecution of the native Christians and though the Treaty Consuls were very unwilling to interfere in a matter not affecting any of their own subjects, yet they were of opinion that they might venture to address a letter of remonstrance to the Governor-General informing him at the same time that they were only actuated by a friendly spirit in taking this step. A copy of this letter is enclosed.

I am unable to account for the severe measures that the Japanese Government intends to take against these poor Christians as they appear to be very peaceable and quiet people and as far as I can learn the Priests have not been interfering.

Mr. Okuma Hachitaro's visit to Hyogo, who left a few days ago in the " Osaka " is, I believe, in connection with the Christians.

Enclosure.

Nagasaki May 12th, 1868.

To His Excellency
The Governor General Of Kiushiu.

From different sources we have been informed that the Japanese Government intends a great persecution of their Japanese subjects who have embraced Christianity.

We have not the least intention to interfere with the rights which the Japanese Governmeut have to exercise over their subjects but think it our duty in the name of humanity and in the most friendly spirit towards the Japanese Government to make earnest remonstrances against a step which certainly would prevent all civilized nations to regard Japan as heretofore, namely, a civilized nation.

The article VIII of the Treaty stating that :—

" Neither Japanese nor Foreigners should do anything that may be calculated to excite religious animosity." and that :—

" The Japanese Government had abolished the practice of trampling on religious emblems " shows that the question was taken into serious consideration at the time when the treaty was made.

We hope that the new Government will not retrograde—doing what has been done centuries ago—at a time when the highest authorities in Japan declare their adhesion to progress.

Again we beg to state that the letter is merely written in a feeling of friendship for the Japanese Government and in the name of humanity.

Being most anxious to have these reports officially contradicted and trust they may prove to be untrue, we will feel sincerely obliged by your favouring us with a reply at your earliest convenience.

We have etc.,

(Signed by all the Treaty Consuls).

REPORTS BY H.B.M. CONSUL AT NAGASAKI

British Consulate,

Nagasaki June 10th 1868

No. 41

SIR :

I had the honour to transmit you in my memorandum of the 14th, copy of a Despatch addressed to the Governor-General signed by all the Treaty Consuls resident at Nagasaki, upon the subject of the persecution of the native Christians and it will be observed by His Excellency's reply, copy herewith enclosed, that it is contrary to the established law of the country to profess Christianity and regarded as a crime, and unless those who have adopted this foreign religion recant and return to the ancient faith of their ancestors, they will be punished in the same way as any other criminal, who infracted the laws of his country.

At a private interview I had with the Assistant to the Governor-General I took the liberty of offering a few suggestive remarks and stated that it would be very impolitic on their part at the present unsettled state of the country to put these measures of persecution into force and trusted that they would delay putting them into execution until I had an opportunity of bringing the matter fully before you, that you might intercede for these poor Christians with the Mikado's Government.

Draft of Translation.

Nagasaki, May 31st, 1868.

GENTLEMEN,

We beg to acknowledge the receipt of your despatch of the 12th instant, with reference to reports which have reached you of severe punishments being about to be inflicted on those Japanese subjects who have embraced the Christian faith.

We respect the humane feelings which dictated this letter, and we pity those perverse minded Japanese of the lower class, who, in the face of an old established Japanese law, have committed the crime of apostatizing to a strange religion, the practice of which is strictly prohibited; but we shall have no alternative but to punish them according to Japanese law if our repeated remonstrances do not cause them ultimately to repent and retract their errors.

You further state that the 8th Article of the Treaty provides that there shall be no religious animosity between Japanese and Foreigners, and that the practice of trampling on religious emblems had been abolished by the Japanese Government. It is true there should be no animosity with regard to the respective religions professed by each country, and both Foreigners and Japanese are at liberty to follow their own.

But the abolition of the practice of trampling on religious emblems had no reference to your country's religion.

You express a hope that the new Government will not revert to obsolete practices at a time when the highest authorities have declared their adhesion to progress, and this gives us great pleasure. It shall be the earnest endeavour of the new Government to avoid any retrograde step, but if we wish to maintain our laws it is impossible to be remiss in the case of persons who have disregarded the strict prohibitions contained in them, and the delay hitherto accorded has been from motives of humanity only.

In the last paragraph of your despatch you ask whether the reports you have heard were true or not; we hope you will clearly understand our answer from what has been said above.

We have etc.,

By order of the Governor General of Kiushiu.

MACHIDA MIMBU
SASAKI SANSHIO
NOMURA SOSHICHI

Trans.
W. G. ASTON.

REPORTS BY H.B.M. CONSUL AT NAGASAKI

No. July 15th 1868.

SIR:

On receipt of your Despatch. No. 28 of the 1st. ult. upon the subject of the threatened persecution of the native Christians, I have the honour to inform you that I took an early opportunity of conferring with the Japanese authorities to find out what their intentions were regarding them and likewise to carry out the instructions contained in your Despatch.

I sought an interview with the Governor-General* but finding that he could not receive me, being indisposed, I was obliged to see his Assistants. I explained to them your view regarding the native Christians and gave them clearly to understand that it was not our desire to interfere in the least in the internal affairs of the country, and used every argument in my power to dissuade them from following a course of persecution which would certainly bring upon them the displeasure of all the Treaty Powers. They took the advice tendered in the same friendly spirit it was intended and promised to communicate it to the Governor-General.

They were not at liberty, they stated, to inform me what proceedings would be taken againt them, the matter being still under discussion.

I received a friendly visit a few days afterwards from Kido Junichiro, a Japanese officer, who was sent to Nagasaki on a special mission by the Mikado's Government and more especially to enquire into the state of the Christians and to make arrangements for carrying out the measures adopted at Miako (Kyoto) regarding them.

After preliminary conversation the subject turned upon the Christians and he then communicated to me the views of the Mikado's Government. He stated that great animosity and

* At this time there was a Governor-General of Kyushiu, resident at Nagasaki.

ill-feeling existed between the Christian population and the Japanese of the lower classes, which eventually they were afraid might lead to disturbances and civil strife between the two parties. The Government therefore considered it their duty to take some precautionary measures to prevent such a state.

It was not so much against Christianity that they were acting but to preserve order in the country. Christianity for what he knew might be a very good doctrine, and if it was the general faith of the country it would not be objectionable, but they had the sad experience of when the Jesuits were here about 2½ centuries ago. For the welfare of the country, he considered it desirable that Christianity should be put down. It was not the wish of the Government to resort to any severe measures and trusted that it would not be necssary; however, if the means they were taking did not effect the desired result, they would be under the obligation of doing so.

Kido Junichiro then stated that it had been decided by the Mikado's Government to distribute at present only 150 of the more confirmed Christians of Urakami among the several Daimios of the country; they would commence in a few days. He estimated the total number, as far as they had been made acquainted, from two to three thousand. There might be many more but they had not openly declared themselves or been confirmed.

The Government undoubtedly do not know the extent to which Christianity has spread, for the French Priests sometime ago assured me that they were aware that the number exceeded forty thousand including women and children. They were not all real Christians perhaps but they had the germs of Christianity in them.

I could observe by the manner in which Kido spoke of these native Christians that the Mikado's Government intended by every exertion in their power to stop the progress of

Christianity among them; even if the present measure of separation had not the desired result, that they intended to resort to more stringent measures and eventually to put some of them to death if after the lapse of time they did not recant and return to the faith of their ancestors. The Government originally intended putting some to death but that they had resisted.

Kido stated that Roman Catholic Priests were regarded with great aversion; to them were attributed the troubles that were beginning. He thought the means they were employing were not very creditable and he believed that they still kept up a secret correspondence with the Urakami Christians. He considered that their presence here was not required and rather objectionable, but he did not see how they could be got rid of.

The definition he gave of a Missionary was—a man who is sent to Japan to teach the Japanese to break the Laws of their Country—I mention this, which I believe is the prevailing opinion regarding the Priests among the better class of the Japanese.

I made the same appeal to the good feelings of Kido Junichiro as I had done a few days previously to the Assistants of the Governor-General in favour of these poor native Christians and endeavoured by every possible argument in my power to dissuade the Japanese Government from entering upon a course which might ultimately lead to very serious conflictions.

He listened with much attention and appeared very much pleased with the friendly advice offered by the British Government but he considered it incompatible with the interest of the country to allow Christianity to spread.

A few days after my conversation with Kido, the expulsion of these poor victims commenced, and on the 10th inst. about 120 were put on board a Japanese steamer in harbour belonging to Kozo. The steamer sailed early the next day, tho' the weather was most unfavourable. I have been since informed that 66 of their number have been sent to Choshiu, 20 to Fukuyama and 28 to Shinano. Upon hearing these facts the Consular Body held a meeting the next day to deliberate upon what was best to be done and we decided upon addressing another letter to the Governor-General in the same friendly spirit as before. (Copy herewith enclosed) to which we have not yet received any reply.

I have been informed from private sources that there is very strong feeling among the better class of Japanese against these Christians and the measures that the Government has put into force are not popular ; they consider they are not half severe enough, and Christians ought to be treated as criminals for breaking the laws of the country.

The animosity may arise from the fact that all of the Christians belong exclusively to the lower class. They are small farmers, farm labourers and artizans.

I have etc.

TO HIS EXCELLENCY THE GOVERNOR-GENERAL.

We the undersigned Consuls of the Treaty Powers resident at Nagasaki have the honour to communicate to Your Excellency that we have been informed that a large number of Christians have been arrested and sent away from Nagasaki on board of a steamer.

From our previous communication addressed to Your Excellency dated the 12th May you will have observed that we take a lively interest in the fate of these poor Christians. We would therefore feel obliged by your informing us the place of their destination and what may be the intention of the Japanese Government respecting them, likewise those that are still remaining at Urakami.

Our motives in making these enquiries are not, as we have stated before, to interfere in the internal affairs of the country, but merely to point out in the most friendly way that any outrage against humanity committed against innocent persons only because they profess the Christian faith cannot but injure the reputation of the Japanese Government in the eyes of the civilized world.

We therefore venture to hope that you will give due consideration to the measures that you deem fit to adopt regarding these native Christians.

We have, etc.,

With respects and considerations.

(Signed by all the Treaty Consuls).

July 11th, 1868.

Translation.

TO THE TREATY CONSULS OF NAGASAKI.

July 17th, 1868.

GENTLEMEN,

In acknowledging your letter of the 11th instant, we beg to say that it is quite true that certain Japanese subjects of the lower class who believe in the Christian religion have been removed from this place in a steamer. Our reason for doing so was that these persons having transgressed our laws, we received instructions from Kioto in accordance with which they have been conveyed to and placed in charge of Mori Saisho, Kamei Oki-no-Kami and Abe Kadzuye-no-Kami.

With regard to the punishment of the remainder, we shall await the instructions which will be sent from Kioto as soon as a decision has been arrived at, but in no case shall any of our innocent subjects be unmercifully punished by our Government.

We return you many thanks for your friendly suggestions, and hope that you will understand the action we have taken.

We have, etc.,

(Signed) SASAKI SANSHIO
NOMURA SOSHICHI
KUSUMOTO

Trans. W. G. ASTON.

Proclamation Issued Against Christianity in 1868.

Art. 1. Although for many years the affairs of the Christian sect were strictly prohibited by the Bakufu, the tainted ones do not disappear. Lately in the neighbourhood of Nagasaki at the town of Urakami some labourers secretly believed this doctrine.

As this sect is gradually spreading, and in consequence of serious consultations, His Majesty expressing particularly gracious intentions has been pleased to command that these matters shall be settled in accordance with the annexed instructions.

Art. 2. Although the said sect was from the commencement very bad, those who take charge of the people forming this sect, shall treat them kindly in order that by teachings their hearts may be changed.

Should they however not repent capital punishment will unavoidably follow, and be inflicted on all who do not accept this way of changing their hearts.

Art. 3. Until such time as their hearts shall have been changed, acquaintances shall hold no intercourse with him.

Art. 4. They shall not only be employed in cultivating the ground, working gold, coal and other mines, but shall also be used as labourers in any capacity.

Art. 5. They shall live in the mountains. (Places where few people live).

Art. 6. During a period of 3 years from the day when they are taken charge of, the necessary provisions will be supplied to the various Daimios. They will gradually, as circumstances will permit, be brought from Nagasaki and the Daimios shall receive the various numbers of persons allotted to them at the appointed places.

These commands having been issued they shall be obeyed without fail.

Yanagisawa Kai-no-kami	about	100	persons
Toda Iosumi-no-kami	,,	156	,,
Tokusawa Motochiyo	,,	250	,,
I'kammon-no-kami	,,	130	,,
Toda Unimi-no-kami	,,	80	,,
Sakai Wakasa-no-kami	,,	80	,,
Matsudaira Echizen-no-kami	,,	150	,,
Aoyama Ukino daibu	,,	50	,,
Matsudaira Dsusho-no-kami	,,	50	,,
Honjo Hoki-no-kami	,,	50	,,
Kii Chiunagon	,,	250	,,
Okochi Giobu Taiyo	,,	50	,,
Mayeda Saicho	,,	250	,,

The preceeding shall be delivered at the Kura Yashiki in Osaka.

Ikeda Inaba-no-kami	about	150	persons
Matsudaira Dewa-no-kami	,,	150	,,
Kamii Oki-no-kami	,,	30	,,
Ikeda Bizen-no-kami	,,	150	,,
Asano Aki-no-kami	,,	150	,,

The preceding to be handed over at Onomichi.

Nakagawa Shiridaibu	about	50	persons
Naito Oinozo-no-kami	,,	50	,,

The foregoing at Nakaosuma.

Matsudaira Kawachi-no-kami	about	80	persons
Abe Kadsuye-no-kami	,,	80	,,

The preceding at Tomodsu.

Ongasawara Toyochiomaru	about	50	persons

The foregoing at Kokura.

Kachis'ka Awa-no-kami	about	130	persons
Matsudaira Sanuki-no-kami	,,	100	,,

The above to be taken delivery of at Marugami.

Kuroda Mino-no-kami	about	150	persons

The preceding at Hakata.

Date Tokomi-no-kami	about	80	persons
Yamanouchi Tosa-no-kami	,,	130	,,

The above at Mitsubano.

Tachibana Hida-no-kami	about	80	persons
Arima Nkato'kasano Taiyu	,,	120	,,

The foregoing at Iwadsuma.

Shimadzu Shirodaibu	about	250	persons

The preceding at Kagoshima.

Hosokawa Echu-no-kami	about	150	persons

The above to be handed over at Takahashi.

Total of 34 Daimios, number of men about 4,100 persons.

From the above letters it is clear that the governing classes of Japan still retained a deep antipathy to Christianity; it is hardly surprising therefore that they considered it necessary to prevent its propagation. Fortunately the Powers resisted the temptation to intervene by force for happily this second persecution soon came to an end, though not before many had died from exposure and want in captivity. Here and there scattered up and down the countryside their tombs may still be seen. Similarly from time to time gravestones of the seventeenth century Japanese Christians have been found, especially in Kyushiu and around Kyoto, where, at Takatsuki nearby, was a strong centre of Catholicism under the Christian Daimyo Lord Justo Takayama, himself an exile to Manila in 1614, where he died a year later. At Nagasaki the sites of most of the former Churches are known. On that of the Church of St. John the

Baptist there still exists the well into which tradition says the bones of the martyrs, relics, holy vessels, etc. were thrown at the time of the first persecution. According to the records of the Honrenji Temple which now stands on the spot, the well was closed up and has never been opened from that day to this. Whether this story be true or not, the present priests of Honrenji still refuse to allow the well to be unsealed fearful that, if it were touched, some disaster might overtake the Temple. The High Priest will also tell visitors how on certain occasions the ghost of an old man dressed in priest's robes appears on the site where once stood the vestry and how persons who attempt to sleep in the chamber adjoining the well find themselves disturbed in the night. In the Temple are kept two oil paintings done on Japanese fusuma or wooden sliding doors, which, it is claimed, formed part of twelve such doors each of which bore a picture of one of the Apostles. The originals are now so faded that it is difficult to make out the subjects ; nor does it seem credible that these pictures should have survived the persecution. Yet in recent years quite a number of Christian gravestones have been discovered in the neighbourhood of Nagasaki, and in the modern Urakami Catholic Cathedral is a small museum of relics such as missals, pictures of saints, medals etc., which have been preserved by the Japanese Christian families and handed down from father to son, being only brought to light after the re-opening of the country. Besides the Church of St. John the Baptist at Honrenji as just mentioned, there were " All Saints " on the spot, where the Shuntokuji Temple is to-day and " San Pablo " and the Jesuit Seminary on the eminence occupied now by the Government offices ; the present Girls' Normal School stands where once stood the Church of Santa Maria and Koenji Temple, where the Dominican Church of St. Augustus used to be. Another school deputises for San Dominic and the old Miserecordia or Charity Hospital was in Motohakata machi. It has always been a moot point as to

Some old Christian Tomb-stones found near Kyoto.

what manner of buildings these Churches were. Were they of stone, like the hundreds of old Churches in the Philippines, or were they of timber? A few words from the Spanish history of Fr. Diego Aduarte makes it clear that some of the Churches were of wood, for speaking of the destruction of one, he mentions how the Fathers had to tear down the Church and find ships "to carry it away, it being all wood built without nails and fitted together." This author by the way ascribes the advent of the first Japanese persecution to the same devil which caused the English Reformation. "A priest" he says, "trying to overcome a person possessed of a devil, made the devil speak; the devil said he was the same that caused so many heresies to occur in England and that he had been sent to make similar disturbances in Japan."

TRANSLATION OF THE INSCRIPTION ON THE MONUMENT OF ITAKURA SHIGEMASA (MIMPO).

" The monument of Itakura Shigemasa, Jûgobon Naizen-no-shô. Corrected by Sentonchku Mimpo."

" The thoughtful, benevolent man in seeking life does not violate benevolence, and in losing his life he is also benevolent. Life and death depend upon heaven, or fate. The man who spares his life and considers his own happiness is a disgrace to the perfect man ; but he who, though seeing danger, disregards his life, acts the part of the perfect man. Therefore, if you wish to do what is right, and put instruction into practice, do not choose between what is easy and difficult ; if you wish to advance and make a name, do not consider what is your advantage and disadvantage. Itakura Shigemasa, Jûgobon Naizen-no-shô was a brave and eminent man. His father Katsushige, Jushibon-Jijin Iga-no-gon-no-kami were successively, father and son, appointed Shoshidai (Shôguns resident at Kioto), and guarded the Emperor's palace. Their honours and praises are spoken of everywhere. In his youth Shigemasa served Lord Tôshô Daijin (Iyeyasu) and assisted in the government. He had a brave heart, was upright and gentle, but decided. He was in the service in turn both of Taitokukô (Hidetada) and Taikenkô (Iyemitsu), receiving no small honours from them. In Teichiu, the fourteenth year of Kanyei (1637), the rebels who had been led astray by Jesus made their headquarters at ' The old castle ', of Hara, in the village of Arima, in the district of Kôrai, in the province of Hizen. The gatherings of these multitudes, like bees and ants, was known in Yedo. Taikenkô, in order to destroy them by the aid of the Daimiôs and samurai of all Kiushiu, gave special orders to Shigemasa that he should take command of the army and superintend the whole affair. Shigemasa took his eldest son and heir, Shigemori, and set out immediately. When he arrived he went about to view the towers and ramparts, the village and country, and from time to time carried out his deep-laid plans. On the first day of the first month of the next year, Shigemasa, in his zeal and courage, rushed impetuously into the midst of the enemy, where his helmet being crushed, and his lance broken, he in the end perished, being fifty-one years old. How deplorable ! how sad ! Shigenori had followed him, and harassing his soul, valiantly put forth his strength, but alas ! victory and defeat are according to fate. 'Taigi died in the rebellion, and Yensai perished in the fortress, and for thousands of years their patriotic zeal and righteous courage have remained untarnished'. And the same will be said of Shigemori. Not long after this the rebellion was suppressed, as it is said, 'One's punishment comes upon him as quick as thunder', and again, 'Is it not true that the strength of a position is overcome from within ? It must be said that this man lost his life in doing worthy deeds. And does not every one turn up his sleeve to wipe the tears on his account ? Genyukô (Iyetsuna) in time of peace appointed Shigenori to office, and he kept the Castle at Ōsaka. After this he was constantly advanced, and was made Shissei (Minister), and had conferred upon him the title of Shushibon. He was appointed Jijin (Lord in waiting) and became guardian of the Castle of Karasuyama in Yashiu. He received an income of five thousand koku, so he made his house famous. His son Jushihon inherited his position and imitated his good deeds. When the present Shôgun (Tsunayoshi) began to reign, he was employed in the government. His income was increased, and he was transferred to the Castle of Iwaki, in the province of Musashi. Behold how each generation advanced by the abundance of good deeds. Shigemitsu set up this monument for Shigemori, on the spot where he fought and died and recording his brilliant deeds, wishes to make them known perpetually. The disposition to remember ancestors and to make them known is filial piety and a pleasure. Shall we call this the monument of peace at Waisei, or shall we call it the monument of weeping at Kenzan? I was asked to write something, to wit, an abbreviation of the most important events, and some poetry which poetry is the following: "--(Here follows the poetry, which is of no historical value).

"The ninth month of the ninth year of Yempo" (1681).

An inscription on the back of the stone is to the effect that Hayashi Fuminari, apparently by direction of Shigemitsu, the hero's grandson, had prepared the above writing, and intended to erect the monument, but was prevented from doing so. However, Sentonchoku (probably a priest) carried out his design in 1791, one hundred and fifty-four years after the rebellion. This was doubtless done by order of Itakura Shigemasa's descendants, whose names are there recorded with their titles, etc.

The Tomioka Monument.

THE TOMIOKA MONUMENT

Near the village of Tomioka in Amakusa, some twenty miles from the " Old Castle ", there is another monument, bearing an inscription in some respects more interesting than those on the battlefield. The stone is an undressed, sea-worn one, about seven feet high, standing upon a slightly elevated grassy mound. The tradition of the place is that Christians of the locality, captured at the " Old Castle ", were brought back to Tomioka, and having been condemned, were decapitated and buried there. The number 3,333, is probably a complete number, or used to indicate a great many. Near the top of the stone is inscribed in a circle a Chinese character, used doubtless as a Buddhist mystic symbol. Beneath this is the statement, that " If any one hears (believes ?) Buddhism, he will of course become a saint " (hotoke). In the same line below are two more mystic Chinese characters. The remainder of the inscription is as follows :—

" The principles of Christianity are mainly established in false doctrine, and have no other object than the seizure of the country. In China, not otherwise than in Japan, this sect has been interdicted. It appears evident that Iyeyasu formerly used severe measures in order to reform the sect, but with dissimulation they cherished evil inwardly, and neither reverenced Buddhism, nor obeyed the laws of the Emperor. In the end they showed their perverse hearts as is related below. Therefore, the Shôgun sent orders to the daimiôs of Kiushiu, and at that time the whole of the sect was destroyed, and the world (Japan) became tranquil. The many ten thousands of their heads were collected, and being divided into three lots, were buried in Nagasaki, Shimabara, and Amakusa. From that time the peace of the whole of Japan was sung, just as ' In the day of Shun, they fanned the breezes of Oio,' Joy ! Joy ! "

" Nirada Shirô, of the district of Amakusa in Higo, of Japan, was a young rebel. He established the Christian sect and made known the false doctrines everywhere. Those men and women only who were disaffected formed the party. In the winter of 1636 they destroyed Buddhist and Shintô temples, burned villages and farm houses, and passed over to the district of Shimabara in Hizen, where they prepared for siege. There were more than 31,000 of them. Their immediate object was to subvert the country. Therefore all the daimios of the land hastened to the battlefield, and by night and day, by sea and land, the fighting did not cease. Finally, at the end of the next spring, they made a breach upon the castle, and slew and captured the evil company, great multitudes. But there was a remnant of the sect not destroyed. In this village of this district, there were three thousand three hundred and thirty-three heads collected and buried, making one grave. The honourable Governor Suzuki Shigenari, a distant descendant of Nomi Daijin Shigetoku, who was the chief of the retainers of Kumano Gongen, being a worthy and estimable person, is moreover benevolent and just, and besides skilled in arms and a man of learning. His Excellency seeing the mound grave of those people, and pitying the many thousand evil spirits wandering in pain, performed the meritorious act of setting up this monument. I earnestly pray that by his good works every one of these spirits may forthwith become a saint (hotoke), and prove the benefit of being purified in hades." (There following four lines of poetry).

" The twenty-fifth of the seventh month of the fifth year of Seihô (1648).

" Written by Priest Chinkaso."

In the village graveyards, connected with the temples, are many tomb-stones of the ordinary shape, but bearing no other inscription than that of a simple circle. These are said to mark the graves of Christians. Such stones are found in the graveyards about Nagasaki also. But no positive proof has yet appeared to show that it was the custom of the Christians to mark the graves of their co-religionists in this manner. However, if it were the custom, the circle with the cipher on the Tomioka monument may be very significant.

INDEX

INDEX

昭和五年六月十五日印刷
昭和五年六月二十日發行

定價参圓五拾錢

著作兼發行者	大阪市北區宗是町英國領事館 エム、パスケー、スミス
發行所	神戸市海岸通一丁目三番 ゼー、エル、タムソン(小賣)株式會社
印刷所	神戸市前町十四番館 株式會社神戸大阪プレス社
印刷者	神戸市前町十四番館 ドーグラス、エム、ヤング
發賣所	神戸市海岸通一丁目三番 ゼー、エル、タムソン(小賣)株式會社

RECENT BOOKS on JAPAN

Published by

J. L. THOMPSON & Co. (Retail) Ltd.

SOME ASPECTS OF JAPAN AND HER DEFENCE FORCES

By Captain M. D. Kennedy

This is a book by a resident in Japan who is a keen student of the life that goes on around him and who has been fortunate enough to be able to view that life from several different aspects. A Captain in the British Army, he was attached to a Japanese regiment as a language officer, and is thus intimately acquainted with the military life of Japan. He was also for a time engaged with a large British commercial firm and is now correspondent for Reuters in Tokyo, a position which gives a unique opportunity for viewing the development of Japan—an opportunity of which the author has made full use. Any student of Far Eastern questions will find the book informative and very interesting. Price: Yen 6.00.

ENGLAND AND JAPAN

With Preface by M. Paske-Smith, C.B.E.

The First Known Account of Japan in English extracted from the "History of Travayle" 1577. This book contains photographic reproductions of the title page of the "History of Travayle" and nineteen pages of text dealing with Japan, originally published in 1577. As the original is in old English and black letter type a modern English version of the text is printed along with the reproduction of the original. Two old maps, one of Japan and one of Nagasaki, are also reproduced. The description given of Japan is of great value, and it is interesting to compare the accounts of customs and characteristics with some of those obtaining at present. Price: Yen 6.00.

NETSUKÉ

By F. M. Jonas

An historical and descriptive account of these fascinating objects of Japanese Art. Profusely illustrated throughout by examples in the collection of the author.

The text comprises 180 pages of letterpress giving a historial review of the subject of Netsuké, and detailed descriptions of the subjects and tales which are depicted by the Netsuké artists. Printed throughout on genuine hand-made paper and handsomely bound in leather.

There are over 213 illustrations on fifty-five plates, on nine of which the subjects are printed in colours. The book is well indexed and contains an appendix giving a list of Netsuké carvers together with the signatures they used and short biographies of the more important carvers.

An excellent guide to owners of Netsuké in deciding the subjects portrayed by their carvings. Price: Yen 25.00.

KAMI NO SHIMA
MIDWAY GUARD
WATCH TOWER
NEZUMI SHIMA
GUARD HOUSES
IWASEDO
NISHI TOMARI
TATEGAMI
MINAGE
EBISU SHRINE
SENOWAKI
No. 1 YADAI
No. 2 YADAI
KANZAKI
OGAMI
TOW BOATS
DESPATCH BOAT
FOOCHOW SHIP
PATROL BOAT
MEGAMI
PATROL BOAT
NANKING SHIP
SHINDAIBA (NEW FORT)
TOMACHI
GUARD HOUSES
UMEGA SAKI
MINAMI SESAKI RICE STORE
WATCH TOWER
CHINESE GUARD
GUARD
MOTO KAGO MACHI
CHINESE RESIDENCES
DAITOKUJI
MARUYAMA
THE MAP OF NAGASAKI
REPRODUCED FROM A JAPANESE MAP OF
JUNE 1802
GIVING THE ANCHORAGES
OF
DUTCH AND CHINESE VESSELS
■ DENOTES THE HOUSE OF A DAIMYO MANY OF WHOM KEPT ESTABLISHMENTS AT NAGASAKI FOR TRADING PURPOSES.
THE SITES OF THE OLD CATHOLIC CHURCHES AND ROUTE OF THE LAST OF THE OLD CATHOLIC PROCESSIONS, WHICH TOOK PLACE IN 1614 HAVE BEEN ADDED IN RED.

KARASU YUWA
(CROW'S ROCK)
GOSHINJI
INASA DAKE
MIZUSHITA
HIEDA
INASA MISAKI
PATROL BOAT
RICE STORES
HIZEN SAGA
SITE OF ST. JOHN THE BAPTIST CHURCH
HONRENJI
SITE OF ALL SAINTS CHURCH
HIRADO MACHI
OMURA MACHI
SHIMABARA MACHI
SHIN MACHI
SAKURA MACHI
HIKIJI MACHI
KAJIYA MACHI
YAWATA MACHI
IMA KAJIYA MACHI